thrive inside™

Transformative Secrets of Spiritual Masters, Gurus & Shamans

Let your dreams fly!
love,
Bill

By Bill Eager

www.ThriveInside.net

Chakra Systems LLC

Library of Congress Catalog Number: 2010906574

ISBN: 1452852111
ISBN-13: 9781452852119

1st printing August 2010

Printed in the United States of America

For Laurie

ACKNOWLEDGEMENTS

I share lessons from teachers whose backgrounds encompass Buddhist, Christian, Hindu, Jewish and Shamanic traditions. They all have an impact on my experience of life. I cannot take credit for anything. These teachings have been passed down through many generations and lineages. I offer to you what has been lovingly given to me. This is the twisted hair tradition. Many paths and directions strengthen each other. Like a braided rope, each thread stands on its own merit. When many threads are woven, twisted together, the rope becomes incredibly strong. With love to all my spiritual teachers past, current and future.

Alan Finger
Alberto Villoldo
Amma Sri Karunamayi
Bapuji
Cheyenne
Eagle
Gurudev (Yogi Amrit Desai)
GrandMaster Choa Kok Sui
Master Stephen Co
Neem Karoli Baba
Paramahansa Yogananda
Sakyong, Jamgön Mipham Rinpoche

Thanks also to Mary Ahlbrandt and Tom Bosma for proofreading, Leilani Henry and Philip Eager for inspiration and dialog and Jennifer Rogers for cover design.

CONTENTS

INTRODUCTION

How This Book Will Help You

This book is about your transformation. You do not create transformation. You experience it. Like a flower bud that reaches the time to open. There is no willful action in blossoming. Change your awareness about yourself. Your conviction about yourself and the world you live in. This is transformation. This is the space we walk in.

I share techniques that help you experience the process of your own transformation. Through conscious transformation you achieve harmony and personal satisfaction in life. The book focuses on transformation in five distinct areas which are common in daily life.

1) Career and finances
2) Relationship with your body and health
3) Relationship with nature
4) Relationships with other people
5) Spiritual development

If you wake up tomorrow and all these areas of your life are in perfect harmony you would be in a state of bliss. You should ask for and expect no less from life. This life is more than ordinary. It is your birth right to have transformational experiences that create harmony and happiness. This is how you change yourself and transform the world.

Transformation is Guaranteed

As I turn south on highway 62-180, heading out of Carlsbad, New Mexico, the land to the east sweeps out in vast fields of grass and yucca plants. Towards the west, the dark blue outline of mountains stands like a paper shadow in the distance. It is hard to tell if they are covered with trees or rock formations. Ahead, the road seems endless. The last gas station and grocery store for more than sixty miles is at the entrance to Carlsbad Caverns National Park.

After buying gas, string cheese, crackers and soup, I continue south into Texas. Suddenly, a wall of stone carpeted with pinion trees rises up like a natural skyscraper. This is Guadalupe Mountains National Park, one of the greatest examples of an ancient, marine fossil reef on Earth. Two hundred and fifty million years ago, during what geologists call the Permian Age, a tropical ocean covered the region. Within this enormous sea, sponges, algae, and lime-secreting marine organisms formed a reef that paralleled the shoreline for four hundred miles.

Once this vast ocean evaporated, the reef was buried in dense blankets of sediment and salt. Entombed like an undiscovered Egyptian mummy until geological movement exposed massive portions. Millions of years of geological transformation mold the skeleton of the Guadalupes; and the timeless persistence of wind and water carve its personality.

Nestled between two honey mesquite trees the size of small shrubs, my green Sierra Designs dome tent fits nicely in the terrain. There are no clouds today. To get a clear view of the night sky I skip putting on the rain fly. Two a.m. I crawl out of the tent for a better view of the stars. The nearest town sits almost one hundred miles away so there is no light pollution. The star field is enormous. Our own Milky Way, with its distinctive, cloud-like appearance, is clearly visible.

Standing below this astral landscape, in a remote wilderness with a geological history that spans millennium, I momentarily lose a sense of time and space that defies what I perceive most of the time. I am alone in a desert that was once a thriving ocean. Looking at stars that have collapsed and exploded; dying long before the light of their existence touches my eyes this very night.

When I am in nature, time takes on this otherworldly dimension. If I am lucky, I drop out of time. This can happen because nature itself does not perceive time like we do. The transformation of oceans and stars moves time outward. It shows how expansive time can be; and how transformation in the macrocosm occurs slowly from a human perspective. Nature is our teacher and our healer. If we listen closely, her wisdom shows how to be stewards of a planet that provides all we ever need.

Guadelupe is also home to a toad named Couch's Spadefoot. Like all amphibians, it breathes through its skin to remain moist. This toad must survive the long dry spells at Guadelupe (most of the year) by living underground. Spadefoot Toads congregate at temporary pools during summer rains to mate and lay eggs. When eggs are laid a race begins. Eggs hatch within three days; and tadpoles reach full maturity in two weeks. Transformation occurs over millennium - and it happens in a millisecond.

Find Your Own Path

I find irony, but not amusement, in the bickering that occurs between individuals of different religions. Imagine two groups of hikers walking up a trail to the top of a mountain. They start at different trailheads. Their paths cross. When they discover they are both going to the top of the mountain, a heated discussion erupts. They appear to be going in different directions. Each group knows with certainty that their path will reach the summit. The other party is moving in the wrong direction and will never reach the summit. This is a only a problem of perspective. They do not recognize that multiple paths may lead to the same location.

Transformation is similar. There are many paths. Each person finds what they need to move forward on their unique path. We do not all need to be in the same place, or even on the same path. We teach each other when we agree; and when we disagree. Honor that. It is your personal experience that counts. Not what you are told an experience should be. Your capacity for personal growth; and the contribution you can make to the shift in global consciousness is unlimited.

Transformation is a Big Word

One synonym for transformation is change. Indeed, transformation implies that we can bring about positive change in our life. When we experience transformation we move from one condition into a new one. The most significant question is whether you want to consciously participate in the process of your own transformation; or simply let it happen.

You do not have to be actively involved in the process of transformation. You might assume that if you are going to go through personal transformation that you have to engage in the process. Or, that the process is under your control. Neither is correct. You can make zero change in your daily habits and the universe will toss events your way that force change and the opportunity for transformation. A relationship begins, or ends. You get a new job, or lose one. You have a health problem, or your health improves.

One of the most astounding transformations in the animal world is the metamorphosis of a caterpillar into a butterfly. A creature with one type of life experience magically transforms in such a way that it has an entirely different life experience.

As a metaphor for perception, the transformation of a butterfly provides a sense of our own capabilities which are hidden by a limited perception of ourselves and the world we live in. The caterpillar crawls along satisfied with it's two dimensional state of existence. It moves forward, backward, left and right ... on one horizontal plane. It does not yet comprehend the third dimension of vertical movement. It does not know that it soon will have wings to fly in all directions. This is the power of transformation.

Butterflies hold a special place as a symbol in mythology. Greek mythology links butterflies to the human soul. The Greek word for butterfly was *Psyche*, which translates as soul. This was also the name for the human lover of Eros (known as Cupid in Roman folklore). When these two figures are depicted together Eros has his own wings. The couple is surrounded by butterflies. The butterfly also symbolizes Christian resurrection. The butterfly disappears into its cocoon, appears dead, and then emerges as a far more beautiful creature.

On the physical level, transformation happens as you read these words. Cells in your body change. Nerve cells, which may last a lifetime, create new pathways as you bring your experiences to bear on the cognition of the words on the page. The epithelial cells that line your mouth live only a few days and may be gone by the time you get to Chapter Four.

Let's begin.

thrive inside

LET SUCCESS HAPPEN 1

I sit in the front row of an energy healing workshop taught by Master Stephen Co of the U.S. Pranic Healing Center. Standing on the dais in a glorious golden shirt, Master Co carries a youthful face and the energy of a teenager. It belies his years of experience as a great healer and teacher. He has already advised me several times, in front of this audience of three hundred, I need to uncross my arms if I expect to understand these teachings. Crossed arms create an energetic shield that blocks communication. Perhaps appropriate in a business meeting, but not in this training. He looks back across the room and asks a simple question, "Does anyone here have challenges with their finances? Raise your hands." I turn around. Three hundred hands point straight up.

It is common for people on a spiritual path to encounter financial problems. Spiritual growth often focuses on the upper energy centers that are in, and above, the physical body. Known as chakras, the upper chakras connect us to processes that have less to do with survival than the lower chakras. It is possible to create an imbalance that does not help pay the bills. A large percentage of people who are not on any spiritual path also have financial challenges.

Financial security is essential for every individual's unique path in life. If you are going to evolve, you need to feel financially secure, and comfortable with your physical health. These two elements – finances and health - are foundations. Keystones that need to be set before you can explore the other aspects of life. If you can't afford to put food on the table, or your health is poor, you will not have sufficient energy to move towards your higher purpose.

This chapter uses intention, with a focus on financial stability, as groundwork before we explore health, nature, relationships and consciousness itself. Intention can be used for many things; but we start with finance. There is no contradiction between financial security and spiritual enlightenment. That is a myth. At the same time, you do not need to live in a mansion to tap into your highest purpose. Let's explore some other myths.

Myth # 1 – The Solution is in the Future

For centuries western culture has meticulously developed systems that focus on the identification of a series of objectives and outcomes accomplished in a specific timeframe. This is the basis of project management. Regardless of whether you consider the current state of global affairs to be good, bad or ugly, the results of this methodology are undeniable. Never before in history have we been able to look in the rear view mirror two generations and view such dramatic change. Unfortunately, we use the same model for personal growth that we use for the growth of society. This creates problems.

Consider the transformation that can occur in your life when you allow yourself to ignore outcomes to measure success. Because of our conditioned training most people use time as a measure for transformation. This is only another way to create a time oriented goal. For example: how many days, weeks, months or years will it take to achieve an ideal weight, obtain a college degree, get married, have children, save enough to buy a house, find a new job, learn a foreign language, resolve a health problem, retire? The laundry list of time oriented "to dos" is a series of outcomes where we predetermine what the outcome should look like, and exactly how long it should take to get there.

We mistakenly try to turn time-bound goals into time-transcendent solutions. Is there anybody who believes that their problem, whatever the problem is – money, health, relationships, or career – is solved where they are? At this moment. Never. We always think we need to move through time and space to solve every problem. This is the problem. We incorrectly believe that in X weeks or months we can achieve a solution. Then we will be happy. It is like this:

MY PROBLEM IS HERE → MY SOLUTION IS HERE

If the use of time to achieve goals created lasting solutions then everyone on the planet should be in a state of ecstasy. After thousands of years of trying, the human species would have it right. Clearly this has not happened. Instead, humankind collectively, and most of us individually, continue to strive for time and outcome oriented solutions to our various issues. Money is almost always at the top of the list.

Myth # 2 – Time Always Produces Positive Results

The fallacy with this approach is two fold. First there is the issue of time itself. How long will it take us (our family, our country, the world) to achieve the outcome we have identified?

The moment that time enters the equation for finances it immediately assumes that we are currently in an untenable situation and we have to wait X amount of time to get to a place that is qualitatively better. We assure ourselves that X amount of time will actually produce the result we are looking for. Financial institutions sell this soapbox to everyone, even as they dramatically prove how flawed the model is. That is why so many people spend so much of their precious life energy striving to save a *nest egg* to achieve *financial independence*.

We all witness how this does not work. Enron, Lucent, Worldcom, AIG, Wachovia, Merrill Lynch, General Motors. How many times have we seen pillars of the business and financial markets suddenly have dramatic declines leaving billions of dollars and untold numbers of shareholders and employees holding the bag? You can always go back to a point in time where most of us would never have predicted the disastrous financial outcome that more time created. It is supposed to go the other way... right?

Financial advisors shower us with historical trends that indicate a long term view will create the positive outcome we are looking for. Yet every company or mutual fund prospectus also clearly states: past performance does not guarantee future results. Time does not always move finances in an upward direction.

Myth # 3 - Someone Else Knows How Long This Will Take

A second aspect of time related to finances that is quite often incorrectly defined is "how long?" How long, for example, will it take to get a new job? Six months. One year. Again there are formulas about how many months based upon salary expectations. Who makes these rules about time? The moment you buy into other people's expectations about how long the process takes to earn or save X dollars, or to get a new job, you instantly move on a path that is in line with those expectations. You create a self fulfilling prophecy. What you need to say to yourself with conviction is "I do not contract to that." You could find, apply for and get the job you want in one week. When your expectations are something other than this you create mental and energetic contracts with yourself that support your expectations.

Myth # 4 – When I Get There I Will Be Happy

This is the biggest misuse of time for individuals and for mankind. You put a big red X on the calendar to mark the date that you will achieve the outcome you dearly desire. You get there. You actually save enough money to buy a Red Ferrari 360 Spider. If you are wondering, that's $273,500 plus tax.

You buy it. It's fast. You look marvelous. Then it occurs to you. Someone might steal the car. You might get a speeding ticket. Now you have new problems. This is going to take more time to fix. The nature of money, and material purchases made with money, is they create a cycle.

The minute you achieve a calendar oriented goal that encompasses getting a physical object you have to start a new calendar. You never achieve the relaxed ecstasy you imagined when you drew the first X on your calendar. You now stand at a point in time with another time-oriented, money-related problem. You never arrive. There has not been a single time in recorded history when someone became enlightened because they completed their to-do list.

The solution is simple, yet challenging. Acknowledge that you can be happy right now. This moment. This is the moment you live in. It deserves more attention than any other moment. This is Eckhart Tolle's *Power of Now*. It is Ram Dass's *Be Here Now*. Ask yourself this question: At this moment, right now, is your financial problem manifesting? Most likely it is not here. Yes, perhaps your checking account is lower than it needs to be. But, in this moment, it does not impact who you are. Let it go.

You will discover how to manifest the upside, the security and the safety, you are looking for. But, it will occur in a different way than you have been taught. Because it should be clear by now that the way we have been taught does not work.

Myth # 5 – Outcomes Are Definitive

Obviously problems occur when we make time a critical element in shaping success. What about the outcome itself? An idea comes to you. Usually ideas arrive spontaneously. Then you cogitate and mull over and refine. And it seems like you've been "thinking about this" for a long time. The original inspiration usually comes rapidly. Like a dream.

Paint a picture, have a party, get a new job, get married, start a business. Beautiful, conceptual, dreams. Then, immediately, you begin to identify outcomes. You take the idea along several pathways in your mind to envision end results that you think you will be pleased with. My painting could be sold. Will it be good enough? How long will it take? How do I find an art gallery? Do I need a contract? How much will I make? The same with jobs. Is this the right career move? How much vacation will I get? How many interviews will I have to do? Will I need to relocate?

Another common aspect of outcomes is that we not only carefully pre-determine what the outcome should look like; we add insult to injury by cogitating all of the negative possibilities. "I really can't paint." "That job is not for me." The crystal ball inside your brain decides why your new direction in life will never work.

It is incredible. You move instantly from a flash of creative inspiration to getting bogged down into all the possible paths that might occur, all the pros and cons, trying ever so hard to determine what a successful, or unsuccessful, outcome should look like. Before you have even gotten out of your chair, done one thing, you create a hundred stories about the outcome. It is the nature of our wild mind to create these stories. Rarely are any of them correct.

The Myth Buster: Do Not Attach Yourself to Outcomes

Imagine that you start on a new path, a journey, with no expectations about the outcome. No predetermined stories. One of the keys to transformation is to learn to perform actions without attachment to the end result. I use the word *learn* because this is a new way of doing things that takes practice. The best way to practice is to start with little projects. Projects where your mind and ego have already determined that they are not important. Go to the grocery store; mow the lawn; decide what to have for dinner. Even these simple tasks take on gravity and story telling under the right circumstances.... like when you are running late.

I am not suggesting you become reckless. Simply, if you loosen up control about a simple process, you start to create a new process for living. Show your mind that it does not have to be involved in every aspect of decision making. That while you occasionally appreciate mental micromanagement; there are times where outcomes improve without buy in from your brain.

Profound things start to happen when you eliminate a predetermined outcome. The first thing that happens is you open yourself to enjoy the process. It is like this. You want to paint your house. You have the paint, the ladders, the brushes and some good friends. If you use a time-bound outcome the house has to be painted perfectly in three days. The entire time you worry about how good a job your friends are doing, and whether it will be done in three days. Drop the outcome and allow yourself and your friends to get into the "zone" and enjoy the process. Then, quite magically, the outcome will exceed your expectations. Let success happen.

Do not attach yourself to any outcome. The other aspect of attachment is *yourself*. As hard as it is to eliminate predetermined outcomes; it may be harder to eliminate yourself from the outcome. The outcome, intended or not, is all about you. From the moment you wake up in the morning to the time you hit the pillow your actions revolve around you. Even when you are doing things for other people it is not uncommon to have your own personal reference point on how things are going.

The underlying issue is that not only do we judge outcomes, we judge ourselves. Financial success has become a significant measure of our success. The more money you have the more successful you are. Right? When you lose a job; can't pay bills; see your 401K drop by forty percent, it does not feel good. Part of that feeling is the fear about the money and the uncertain future that arises when your economic position changes. But there is another aspect to the feeling which relates to self esteem. Your financial wealth, and the security blanket you pretend it provides, has an impact on how you feel about yourself and your life.

When this feeling is multiplied by hundreds of millions of people we collectively create a sense of panic and malaise that spreads like a grass fire. The media picks up on the consensus and fuels the flames.

NEW YORK (CNNMoney.com) -- Nearly six out of ten Americans believe another economic depression is likely, according to a poll released Monday.

Of course they call it a depression ... we are depressed. A significant part of this depression starts with a personal sense of who we are and our current state of relative success. This is often in direct proportion to the size of our bank account. And, even when our definition of success is not tied directly to the bank account, as in "I am a successful athlete" or "I am a successful mother" there is usually a side story about money.

If we are successful then we feel good. If we are not successful, not economically bountiful, we start to get down on ourselves because we feel we are doing something wrong. Over the course of life we go through cycles where we see ourselves as successful - or not successful. We might even silently say to ourselves: "I am a success." Or, "I am a failure." Well, which one are you? Success or failure?

Allow yourself the opportunity to go beyond the transient label of SUCCESS or FAILURE, especially with connection to money. Deeply recognize that as a spirit on this planet you are far more than these labels. If you learn to hold your own space of personal value, then what the rest of the world labels as success becomes irrelevant.

Create Your Intention

An intention is not a goal, nor is it an outcome. It is bigger, and more profound. It is a direction, a roadmap, that points the way to significant and sustainable transformation. There are several ways to distinguish a goal from an intention. Goals are time oriented. They have an end-point. With goals, the present moment is an obstacle. When you are goal oriented you create attachment to a specific end result. This attachment creates a conflict between where you are today, at this moment, and where you imagine you will be when the goal is reached. Goals create expectations and stress. In your mind you image how things will be (different) when a goal is reached.

Intentions are timeless. With an intention what happens during the process is more important that what you get, or when you get it. With intention you move in a chosen direction but you are not attached to the outcome. You enjoy yourself on the journey. It is the process that creates transformation, not the end result. With a goal what you hope to achieve is the focus. With intention *you* are the focus. Your intention creates a shift in your thinking and your habits that change how you perceive the world. With a new lens, you change what happens.

In other words, you must have in the beginning what you want in the end. If you want peace in the future you must start with peace now. Your intention is peace. You become peaceful now. You carry peace into your life. How can you possibly become something in the future that you are not right now? It is impossible in both theory and practice. If you push it out to the future when do you get there? Never. If you want peace - be peaceful. If you want love - be loving. These are your intentions. When you create a simple, clear intention, the time-oriented goals for transformation automatically become apparent. It will be a no-brainer (literally).

GOAL: uses future tense, requires external validation, selfish rather than expansive.
INTENTION: is oriented to the present tense, relies on wisdom and guidance from within, involves others in an act of co-creation.

How do you create an intention? Here is a simple, three-step process.

STEP 1
Make a list of five things in your life that create stress. These are events, people, situations, concerns that trigger stress and unease. Put them in order with number one being the most stressful and so on. Here is an example:

1. I am worried I won't have enough money.
2. My friends won't appreciate me if I don't spend time with them.
3. My health problems are a burden for my family.
4. I get upset when people criticize me or my ideas.
5. My physical appearance needs to improve before others will love me.

STEP 2

Focus on your primary stressor (number 1) and make a second list of issues that you believe you consciously, or unconsciously, have with this stressor. In this example: Why am I worried I won't have enough money?

1. Fear of losing what I have.
2. My self esteem is tied into my finances.
3. I hate the idea of not being in control.
4. I need to provide for my family.
5. I don't feel worthy to make a significant amount of money.
6. My parents always had money problems.
7. I have a belief that money corrupts.
8. I equate money with success.

Drill down to core issues that surround and often create the external circumstances of your life. This requires brutal self-honesty. It may require asking a loved one to sanity check your list. Ultimately, everything that you are afraid of is about yourself. As a result you are in the best position to make a sustainable change. This list can provide the foundation to create life-long, not goal-oriented, intentions around the topic of money (or other areas of your life).

To be clear let's review examples of time-oriented, financial goals:
- Pay off two hundred dollars on my credit card this month.
- Get a raise this year.
- Make enough money to buy a new car.

STEP 3

Write down your intention statement. You can have more than one. Here are examples of *financial intentions* that use the underlying issues identified to change the internal belief system and create transformation:

- I release my judgmental perceptions about money that create stress, tension and fear.
- I completely accept myself even though I do not feel worthy of great wealth.

- I openly accept and rejoice in the abundance and riches the universe showers me with.
- I am at peace. I accept myself as I am, and the entire world as it is.

This work aligns your internal intentions with external activities so they can work in harmony. Success really is inside first, outside second. This process creates lasting happiness as your intentions reinforce who you are and your purpose in this life.

For example, if you are worried about money, then reading headlines of newspapers or watching television when they discuss financial disasters that are out of your control could be disturbing. However, if your intention is to be at peace with the world as it exists, then you empower yourself to be calm in the midst of external chaos.

Intention is a mental device you use to create energetic alignment between what you think, say and do. The result is integration in your personal and professional life. Transformation occurs at a deep level where your subconscious mind accepts your intention. You give your intention over to your subconscious mind and your higher self. You become your intention and your intention moves you in the right direction without being confined by results.

Use Intention to Create a New Reality

It is pitch black at four in the morning as my wife and friend Rock rustle around the campsite. They are preparing to summit Mount Shavano. With an altitude of 14,229 feet, it is the seventeenth highest peak in Colorado. The state boasts fifty-four fourteen thousand foot plus mountains. Mount Shavano is also renowned for the Angel of Shavano. The angel is a snow formation in the image of an angel that appears on the east face of the mountain every spring when the snow melts.

My job today is to stay at camp and ensure that a bottle of chilled Chardonnay is ready when the climbers return. As they tie their boots I decide to try a kinesiology experiment. Using my left arm as a guide I muscle test for the exact time they will summit. I randomly test 11:30. No. 12:30. No. 11:45. Stronger. I narrow down the time to 11:56. As Rock slides a final water bottle into his pack I announce my prediction. Late in the afternoon I sit under an aspen tree admiring the shifting patterns leaves create as they dance in the wind. Rock drops his pack onto the ground with a loud sigh. The first thing he says, "Eleven fifty-eight."

One technique for setting intention into the subconscious mind involves kinesiology. Kinesiology is the study of muscles and the movement of the human body. It also encompasses the energetic interaction between our physical body and our subconscious state of mind. Kinesiology uses muscles as a vehicle to connect with the electrical currents that run throughout the body. Muscle responds to truth. Therefore, kinesiology is a technique that allows you to access truth in your personal life. And, it empowers you to tap into the wisdom of the cosmic consciousness. That is why I was able to get so close with my prediction of the time they would reach the summit. If I had used my logical, thinking mind, I would have created a far less accurate prediction.

Wouldn't it be fantastic if you could make your intention list, read it, and be done? Well, it is almost that simple. When intentions align with what you truly desire they have the power to become reality instantaneously.

There is one very important element. You need to solidly set your intention within your subconscious mind. The subconscious mind is like the giant mass of ice that sits below the tip of an iceberg. It is much larger that what we see on the surface, yet we barely acknowledge its presence or power. Until all aspects of your being fully accepting your intention, you will see limited results.

Yoga Nidra is a powerful technique for securing your intention. Known as the "deep sleep of the yogis", Yoga Nidra creates a state of conscious relaxation. Your brain waves actually move into the alpha state of 7 to 12 cycles per second, which is much lower than the normal waking state characterized by beta brain waves of 14 cycles per second. In the Alpha Brain Wave State you actually remember better because you listen energetically. Intention is carried into the deepest aspect of your being. When you are in this alpha state you are open to suggestion as your conscious, logical mind loses it's defensive barriers. When you are in this state you can program your own mind.

Yoga Nidra uses intention as a mental device to create energetic alignment between what you think, say and do with the powerful capabilities of your subconscious mind. A proper experience of Yoga Nidra requires that you be guided either in person, or with an audio CD, into this extraordinary state of consciousness where you drop your intentions into your subconscious mind. The most profound experiences I have had as participant and teacher has been with the Amrit Method™ of Yoga Nidra, created by yoga master Yogi Amrit Desai.

Water as a Vehicle for Intention Setting

Approximately 70 percent of your body is water. You are a walking sponge. Muscle consists of approximately 75 percent water; fat and bones are made up of about 50 percent water. Before you became a walking sponge, you floated effortlessly like a jellyfish in amniotic fluid as a fetus in your mother's womb. Amnion grows and fills with water about two weeks after fertilization. By ten weeks this liquid wonderland contains proteins, carbohydrates, lipids, phospholipids and electrolytes. This maternal energy drink is constantly being inhaled and exhaled. In fact, it is critical that amniotic fluid be taken into the lungs (even though it is not air) by the fetus in order for lungs to develop normally.

Water also plays an essential role in the transformational process. Before we learn a simple technique for using water as a vehicle for intention setting we need to examine and understand the mystery of water to discover its special place as not only a critical life giving substance, but also one of the best vehicles for assisting with transformation.

Just like the human body, 70% of the earth's surface is covered in water. Perhaps this is not a coincidence. Water has many attributes. Two of the most important are A. it transforms easily (ice, water, steam) and B. it moves. Snowmelt becomes streams which flow into oceans where evaporation creates clouds that create rain and snow. The process is so simple, it's perfect. Let's examine a model that illustrates the importance of water and will help you as you engage in transformation.

The Shamanic Wheels of Life

One useful model comes from shamanic traditions. A shaman is someone who studies, teaches and understands what can best be described as "earth wisdom." Almost all indigenous peoples have individuals who are shamans. For thousands of years shamans have studied the cycles of nature on the planet and in the stars.

The models we want to consider are shamanic wheels or circles. Without beginning or end, the circle is not only a metaphor; but also a system that is repeated in nature many times. Planets circle the Sun. Trees have circular rings that record their growth. Hurricanes create vortexes that are circular. The seasons cycle in circles. Shamanic wheels are blueprints or keys to understanding the natural world that we both live in and are part of. A shamanic wheel provides definition and understanding of a certain set or group of physical, mental, emotional, spiritual entities.

Wheels are related to physical directions, just like on a compass. Everyone is familiar with the eight basic directions on a compass: North, Northeast, East, Southeast, South, Southwest, West, Northwest. This is one type of wheel. It is a wheel of directions.

Another wheel you may be familiar with is that of Earth, Water, Air and Fire. Dating back to pre-Socratic times, the Greek classical elements consisted of these four plus a fifth they called Aether. Aether, or ether, refers to the fifth element of space.

In today's highly technological society we often ignore the ongoing relevance of these elemental forces. They are so obvious we don't see them. On the most basic level we contain all the elements in our own bodies. Earth becomes all of the vegetables that we consume. Water and air are required on a daily basis. Fire is the internal combustion that occurs within our body. And space exists within every atom of our being.

Layering the five elements over the compass wheel creates this model:
NORTH = Air
EAST = Fire
SOUTH = Water
WEST = Earth
CENTER OF CIRCLE = Space

Now we create another wheel that can sit on top of this wheel. Air is mental. Fire is spirit. Water is emotions or tears. And Earth is the physical body. You can see how this wheel fits individuals. Do you know someone who is extremely mind oriented? A scientist, engineer, or doctor. They have certain air like qualities. Sometimes when they speak they are literally "over your head." What about people who are full of spirit. Temperamental and full of fire. Others have strong emotional and physical attributes.

In Ayurveda, the ancient Indian science of life, every person has attributes that place them into one (or more) of three categories or doshas. Vata, pitta and kapha. Vata people are naturally more ether and air (north). Pittas are fire (east). And people with Kapha tendencies have more earth and water (south and west). These models definitely work.

NORTH = Mental
EAST = Spiritual
SOUTH = Emotional
WEST = Physical

For humans, water represents emotions. Of all the animals on the planet, emotions are unique to humans. Don't say, "what about laughing hyenas?" They don't count because they are not really laughing. Of all the species on the planet, why do we have emotions? Like water, emotions are about movement and cleansing. Experiencing emotions is critical for personal transformation. But more than just having any one specific emotion (there are a lot of different emotions and levels of intensity) emotions teach us who we are, where we have been and what we need to learn to move forward.

Another term for spiritual light is "living water." When we allow emotions to move through us like water and do not get attached to the emotion itself (or the person or event that caused the emotion) we transform our life. Humans want to experience and know emotions. But we do not want be ruled by emotions. Consider emotions to be agents of change, like flowing water, rather than obstacles. When we don't allow emotions to move and flow rapidly they get stuck inside our physical body. This creates a roadblock that has to be cleared out. Like a rock that needs to be pulled out of a stream before the water can move freely.

There is one more wheel that illustrates the power of water. It is the wheel of the stars, sun, moon and earth. It looks like this:

NORTH = Stars
Guardians. Seeds, a spark of consciousness through time.
EAST = Sun
The Scout. Illuminates time, scouts time, it allows us to see time.
SOUTH = Moon
Provider. It gives us our time (28 day cycle), provides time and creates the waves.
WEST = Earth
Keeper. It stores time. It records time.

The gravitational attraction of the moon creates tides in the ocean. Notice how in the wheels South represents water, emotions and the moon. They all create movement. This movement of water enables us to change our lives. These basic shamanic wheels can be used for other avenues of self exploration. For example, if you meditate it is advisable for best results to do so in the morning facing east. Remember: EAST represents fire, spirit and sun.

EXERCISE

Drink Your Intention

Clearly, water plays an important role in the human experience. Is there a way to use this knowledge? Absolutely. A quart (or a litre) of water moves through your body in approximately two hours. This is water's quality of movement. As such it is a great carrier and it can move and impart an energetic imprint in your body (including your mind and subconscious).

Water becomes both a storage and transmission vehicle to transfer the information of your intention throughout your physical body. You use your body's water content as a medium to introduce new information that changes your body chemistry at the molecular level. The way we are going to accomplish this is quite interesting.

The film *What the Bleep Do We Know* introduced many people to the scientific experiments of Dr. Masaru Emoto. His book, "*The Hidden Messages in Water*" details experiments whereby the molecular structure of water is changed with different sounds and pictures. In a similar fashion we are going to use a quartz crystal and your intention to program water. The hexagonal structure of quartz crystals can rearrange the flexible structure of water. The surface tension of crystal soaked water reaches values that are similar to that of re-energizing devices like batteries.

For this exercise you need to find or purchase a rose quartz crystal. They are common and inexpensive. One that will fit into the palm of your hand is best. When you have this crystal you will first need to clean it. Energetic cleaning will remove any unwanted programming that the crystal contains. Fortunately this is easy to do. Take a glass of salt water. Put your crystal in the water and leave it for twenty four hours. If you can, put the glass with the crystal in direct sunlight.

Now you have a clean crystal. Next you are going to fill a new glass with water. Simple tap water is fine but if you have other water that's o.k. also. Before you go to bed take the crystal and squeeze it in the palm of your left hand. Say your intention out loud. Really focus your attention, your thoughts, on your left hand and the crystal that it holds. Repeat your intention three times. Put the crystal into the water. Now, drink half the glass of water. Go to bed.

In the morning, when you wake up, drink the other half of the water. Take the crystal out of the glass and hold it in your right hand for at least a minute. More if you want. Repeat your intention again. You don't have to do anything special here, just be open and see if you receive any insight. Repeat this procedure for ten days. Watch and see if during this period of time the intention that you "programmed" into the crystal and the water is beginning to take shape in your life.

A Spider Web of Grace

One of my favorite stories comes from *Autobiography of a Yogi* by the great yogic master Paramhansa Yogananda. At one point his teacher, Master Sri Yukteswar, asks whether Yogananda will get an astrological armlet to help with a medical problem. Yogananda replies that he does not believe in astrology. His teacher explains that it does not matter what you believe. It only matters if it is true. To make the point he notes that the law of gravity worked as well before Newton declared it as after; and that the cosmos would be chaotic if its laws could not operate without the endorsement of human belief.

Belief, of course, can play a powerful role in how quickly and how significantly we can change our lives, especially our physical health. Yet the concept is clear. It does not matter whether you believe something for it to work. Often our belief system is out-of-tune, or does not accept, something that we do not understand or have not had personal experience with. If a technique or system has proven it's merit over thousands of years with millions of participants, then it probably will work whether you believe it or not. When we have a personal experience in a matter, we are suddenly more open to sharing the experience and results. This is transformation.

Yogananda's teachings, healings and inspiration continue to travel soundly around the globe. I meet Alan Finger at a yoga retreat in Chicago. The class is already underway when I quietly enter. I see a few spaces in the back of the room. But there is also one good space right in front of the teacher. Without hesitation I move into this space. Immediately I know that Alan is a great yogi. His lecture is wonderful; but it is his energy that grabs my attention. He is totally present. After the class I ask his assistant if I can follow up and possibly meet Yogiraj at some future time. She writes down Alan's cell phone.

Two months later I use the number to connect with Alan and set up an appointment to meet him in New York City where he has an office at Yoga Works, a series of yoga centers that he founded years earlier. When I visit, he has a space where he offers private consultations. I was born in Manhattan. I have worked in this city. Yet I remain amazed at the intensity and variety of sound. New York is a continuous, thunderous symphony that you simply can not avoid.

As I walk into Alan's building the noise of Manhattan begins to shed. When the elevator door opens at his floor, I am instantly transported into a serene space where muted colors and wooden floors evoke a feeling of warmth and nature. I spend about two hours with Alan. We talk. He asks me questions. I lie down and close my eyes. Alan performs energy work. I leave feeling alive, energized and at peace with the intensity of the Big Apple.

Over lunch Alan tells me a fascinating story. His father, Kavi Yogiraj Mani Finger, was born in a Jewish family, and became a great teacher and guru. When Mani was only six, living in South Africa, Gandhi met him and predicted that he would follow a spiritual path. He met Yogananda in 1949 in Los Angeles. Mani Finger would go on to live with Yogananda, and receive Kriya initiation. Alan tells me that it was also predicted that his father would have a son who would become a great yogi. Alan. Today, Yogananda touches me through this lineage and teachings. There is an enormous spider web filled with grace and abundance available for every one of us. You are already on the web.

Sharing Abundance in Life

One of the lasting myths is that there is not enough. Never enough land. Never enough money. Never enough oil. Never enough food. The concept of scarcity is the foundation for growth of nations and corporations. It's easy to understand why. Supply and demand. If scarcity exists, or is created, then the owner of the scarce item creates and owns something of value that others need. The owner prospers.

This theory of *it's mine* not *yours* continues unabated. Under the guise of "Arctic 2007", two Russian mini-submarines travelled to the depths of North Pole's seabed, where a robot arm planted the Russian flag. The symbolic gesture, along with geologic data gathered by expedition scientists, was designed to substantiate Moscow's claims to more than 460,000 square miles of the Arctic shelf. By some estimates the earth below the ocean may contain 10 billion tons of oil and gas deposits. This expedition was done publicly in full view of Russian state-run media. Afterwards, Canadian Foreign Minister Peter MacKay said the Russians are fooling themselves if they believe they can simply lay claim to the Arctic. "You can't go around the world these days, dropping a flag somewhere. This isn't the 14th or 15th century." But it is.

If everyone on the planet always had enough of everything we would have to embrace a new model for everything from the way that companies grow to the manner in which nations expand and interact with each other. Tomorrow morning we wake up and discover that Earth Number Two has suddenly appeared only a short shuttle trip away. Who believes this discovery would instantly solve our fears about scarcity; or the way that we distribute food, energy, water, shelter? We could have ten planet Earths and still it would not be enough.

I am not suggesting something as insane as socialism or communism. These models have not only proven that they do not work; but that they are ultimately similar to capitalism in the unequal distribution of everything with an undercurrent of fear and greed. **I am simply stating there actually is enough of everything.**

I watch hummingbirds. I have two large glass feeders. I discovered that two feeders can attract more of these amazing little birds than one feeder. There are ten little hummingbird seats where they can perch and drink their favorite cocktail - sugar water. I fill both feeders. Enough sugar water for about a week. Two dozen hummingbirds live and roam around the trees near my house. As evening sets in they start to flock to the feeder to get in a nightcap. I sit in their midst, watching. It is amazing. With wings beating at the rate of 3,180 times a minute, twenty-four Ruby throated hummingbirds collectively create the sound of a Blackhawk helicopter. A bird lands at the feeder and within a microsecond another bird flies in to chase away the feeding bird. In fact, most of the time, the hummingbirds never even make it to the feeder. About a foot before landing, they are attacked by one of their own.

Of course they aren't really attacked. It is an outstanding display of posturing. I have never seen a hummingbird actually skewer another bird. It's a crazy scene. Like a busy airport where no plane ever lands. All of this hard work keeping other birds from feeding takes up about 90 percent of their time and energy. Yet, all the while, there is plenty of food for everyone.

Aren't we similar? The abundance of the universe offers us all of the food, air, clothing, and yes, energy we all need to live happy lives. Our sun with it's ongoing nuclear fusion process converting hydrogen into helium and energy sends down to us an astonishing 400 trillion, trillion watts per second. How much is this? In just one second our sun produces enough energy for almost 500,000 years of the current needs of civilization. Clearly there is enough energy.

Tap into Abundance

Since the days our ancestors were hunter-gatherers we have been conditioned with fight or flight responses to many situations. Scarcity triggers it. As individuals and as a species we do this out of habit. Out of fear. We remain ignorant that abundance for every human being on the planet sits before us. Global population growth is a stressing factor that we inadvertently use to intensify a recurring cycle of fear and greed.

There are several aspects of abundance that we need to understand before abundance can come directly into our own lives. They are related. One aspect relates to your personal relationship with scarcity and abundance. How you are feeling. If you have any personal fears based on sensing a lack of abundance you need to recognize these fears and release them.

In fact you may not be aware of a fear a scarcity that resides within your subconscious mind. These fears build up from experiences of one or more lifetimes. When we subconsciously worry about money, or health, or relationships, it creates an internal tension. When we release the energy attached to these negative thought forms we feel physically lighter. We are able to move forward in life as we set positive intentions into our subconscious mind. This helps open the energy channels within and around the physical body that prevent us from both seeing and acting upon abundance.

When you have fears, or don't feel worthy of abundance, you will not even see opportunities that come to you. They can't enter your chakras and you literally won't see, hear or be aware of them. In other words, you could be talking with a friend at a coffee house and they can be sharing a piece of information that could be a perfect solution to your money problems and you would not hear it.

Don't judge yourself. Just be honest and try to discern if you have issues with recurring thoughts that say you either don't have enough, or won't have enough, or might not have enough. Then, use your intention to create internal harmony around this issue. This is a secret to opening the door to abundance.

The Universal Law of Attraction

Your relationship with scarcity and abundance (two opposites) is a manifestation of the Universal Law of Attraction. The equation is profound, yet not complicated. You give energy to what you love. And, you give energy to what you hate. This is very important. You attract into your life all the things, events, circumstances and people that you give energy to.

You may not attract what you want or desire; but you will certainly attract what you are inside. If all day long your internal dialog, you personal mantra, is something like, "I do not have enough. This really sucks. What am I going to do?" Guess what happens? Know without doubt that abundance is available. If you have a mind set of abundance you will attract opportunities into your life that will create the economic situation you desire.

Another aspect of personal abundance that is closely knit with the magnetic is your own level of sharing. The universal law of Giving and Receiving is the essence of prosperity. It is through giving that you prosper. When you give and expect nothing in return, this ensures that you actually do receive something. Put succinctly, what you give you get. In this respect the universe is like a giant mirror that reflects everything you show to it. The first thing you need to do is recognize that the reflection is yours.

The universe provides us what appear to be an endless set of paradoxes. You lose your job, are down and out, and can't pay the bills. Clearly this is not the time you feel abundant. But it is the time when you need to feel most abundant. Similarly, when your own personal economic situation is tight you need to feel un-tight. It is not the time you feel like opening all those non-profit direct mail pieces and pulling out your check book. But this is the time you should. Giving not only should come from your heart; it should be directed towards causes that resonate with you, including your spiritual teachers.

Ebenezer Scrooge shows us how this works. At the beginning of Dickens famous tale: "Oh! But he was a tight-fisted hand at the grindstone. Scrooge, a squeezing, wrenching, grasping, scraping, clutching, covetous old sinner!" After his transformation, helped along by three well known spirit guides: "His own heart laughed: and that was quite enough for him." That large mirror aiming at us is brutally honest. To receive abundance you must believe in it; and give directly from your heart no matter what your current (and fleeting) circumstances.

The Spirit of Creation

Accepting and sharing abundance are the spark plugs that get things going. Most people have an inborn desire to create. The possibilities for creation are infinite. It includes architectural masterpieces over the ages like the great pyramids of Giza, the Eiffel Tower or Beijing's National Stadium nicknamed the "Bird's Nest." It includes traditional African houses made of stones and tree branches known as rondavels, and sand castles that are constructed with tender joy and melt as the tide rolls in. Literature ranging from Shakespeare's finest to daily blogs written by millions of people around the world. From scientific discoveries and technological wonders to a simple cup of tea. One of the fondest human creations is the birth of children.

One magical aspects of being an incarnated soul is that we have the incredible ability to move a dream from un-manifest form into existence. In this respect, as creators, we mirror on a micro-level what nature, and god, accomplish on a larger scale.

One of the reasons we exist in human form is to experience what it is to be the creator; to be intimately involved in the experience of creation. You get close to the creator when you create. Yogi Amrit Desai says it succinctly: "You are the creator. What you believe you create. What you create you become."

There is a dynamic between creator and creation. Indeed, the creator is not separate from his, or her, creation. They are one and the same. As creations ourselves, we encompass divine nature and divine powers. One of the greatest abilities the universe bestows on us is the power of creation. This power comes wrapped in the inseparable forces of energy and consciousness. When we actively and consciously create our lives, we realize the unique purpose of our life on this planet.

Notes and Experiences

ACCESS HEALTH AND HEALING 2

The jungle remains thick. I look up and glimpse a patch of blue sky weaving down through the canopy. I speak freely and openly with my guide Francisco as we walk towards remote Temple IV in the massive complex that is Tikal. Farther away from the main complex with many buildings, Temple IV was built by Ah Cacau's son around 741 AD. It towers 212 feet above the jungle floor. This makes it the tallest structure in North America prior the construction of skyscrapers in the late 1800's. I reach the Temple and climb countless stone stairs to look across the top of an endless jungle.

Francisco, it turns out, is not an ordinary guide. He has spent the past twenty years studying the plants in his native Guatemala. He knows the medicinal properties of more than 112 species and has 750 more to learn. He is also a Mayan Sun Keeper. Out of six million people, the elders have selected him; and given him this title and responsibility.

As we walk I learn more about Francisco, his knowledge and beliefs. "You see this tree," he says, pointing to a large tree with smooth, brown bark and white spots. I nod. "The leaves of this tree can be used to make a medicine that eliminates many types of stomach pain." I reach out to reverently touch this healing tree. He continues, "I make it a point to learn as much as I can about all plants. It is wisdom passed down through generations. And it is for all the people. The plants are here to cure illnesses that the people get."

I recognize the truth in his words. Nature, as a representation of universal wisdom, comes with built-in remedies for many of the specific illnesses and diseases that occur in any region of the world. Of course if most medical problems can be cured for free, or inexpensively, it puts a serious dent in the economic model of the modern healthcare system. Francisco makes this point as he hands me a leaf, "You must understand that the greed of corporate and political systems takes power away from individuals. This enslaves us. Pharmaceutical companies create drugs which are both expensive and addictive. The plants in nature have all of the same miraculous powers."

The life of the ancient Mayans revolved around the concept of time. Priests were consulted on civil, agricultural and religious matters, and their advice would be derived from readings of sacred calendars. Time was of such importance that children were even named after the date on which they were born. The Mayan calendars were derived from those of their predecessors, the Olmec, whose culture dates back 3,000 years. Without the instruments of 16th century Europe, these Central American locals managed to calculate a solar year of 365.2420 days, just 0.0002 of a day short.

I am interested in how the ancient and modern Maya achieved such incredible scientific insights without modern equipment. I ask Francisco, "How did the Maya acquire this incredible knowledge?" He smiles as if he has been waiting to share this with me. "It is because the most important aspect of the universe is order. Behind everything there is incredible order. This is what the Maya study and understand." He pauses and becomes silent. "Look there," he whispers pointing straight overhead. A large toucan sits perched on a branch high above our heads.

The Universe Always Moves Toward Order and Harmony

To the ancient Mayans the universe followed very specific patterns with incredible order. If you knew these patterns with precision then every action could work in harmony with the larger gyrations of universe. Like small wheels turning inside a much larger, precision clock.

They were so familiar with universal laws that they could actually instruct a couple on the exact time to have intercourse if they wanted their child to become an architect, shaman, farmer or any other profession. They knew the timing would coincide with the predisposition of the individual soul to the level of specific vocation. That is serious clockwork.

We have long since forgotten, abandoned, or otherwise ignored these principles. What remains as true today as it did thousands of years ago is that the universe, and nature in particular, strive to achieve a level of order and harmony that far exceed our mental and scientific constructs.

The laws of nature that are most significant for healing purposes are those of Harmony and Order. Order is aligned with Harmony. It stands behind it. Like a giant jigsaw puzzle, order represents the fact that there are an infinite number of pieces which all interconnect to create a vast panorama. Harmony is when the pieces are actually placed together and the image starts to appear.

This relationship between order and harmony may become clearer if we consider insights of famous philosophers and scientists. In his 1902 lecture *The Reality of the Unseen*, philosopher William James described religious life as consisting of "... the belief that there is an unseen order and that our supreme good lies in harmoniously adjusting ourselves thereto."

In his book, *The World As I See It*, Einstein wrote: "The scientist is possessed by the sense of universal causation. His religious feeling takes the form of a rapturous amazement at the harmony of natural law, which reveals an intelligence of such superiority that, compared with it, all the systematic thinking and acting of human beings is an utterly insignificant reflection."

Nature Provides Healing Wisdom

As a species, humans continue to feel and create separation from nature. We talk about "being in harmony with nature" as if there is actually an alternative. Nature is always in harmony. Humans, on the other hand, are not. If human activities create global warming that dramatically shifts conditions for life on planet Earth, nature will neither be disappointed, nor pleased. Nature will simply take these new conditions and move ever forward to a new state of harmony and order. Harmony and order are the underlying foundations for perfect health. The very essence of nature is perfect health. Thus, both the planet we live on, and our individual bodies are designed to be in a state of health.

If this is true then why is the planet we live on, and such a large percentage of the human population, physically ill? The answer partially lies with the lens that we use to view ourselves; and the history of the medical system that has been adopted by most societies.

Ancient and aboriginal societies, like the Mayans, saw the relationship between nature and man as one in which harmony as the natural state, could always be established. Shamans are individuals who learn and respect the traditions of the earth. The divine, feminine energies that rise from what is appropriately called Mother Earth. For a shaman, being killed by a virus is no different than being killed by a grizzly bear. A western doctor would say that the virus is an illness and the grizzly bear is an accident. The shaman, on the other hand, knows that in both cases death occurs because the individual is not in right relationship with nature. To achieve harmony, a shaman seeks an active dialog with the forces of nature.

Even Hippocrates, the Greek physician considered the Father of Modern Medicine, believed that the human body should be treated as a whole and not as a series of discrete parts. Born 460 B.C., Hippocrates accurately described symptoms of many diseases including pneumonia and epilepsy in children. The Hippocratic Oath acknowledges that health and healing go beyond simple diagnostics. Upon graduation, many medical students take a modern version of the oath written by Louis Lasagna in 1964. It states in part: "I will remember that there is art to medicine as well as science, and that warmth, sympathy, and understanding may outweigh the surgeon's knife or the chemist's drug. I will not be ashamed to say "I know not," nor will I fail to call in my colleagues when the skills of another are needed for a patient's recovery."

Western Medicine Takes Root

Coming into the world five weeks premature, I might not be alive to write this book without the intervention of Western medicine. Centuries of advancement in analytical-based medicine have created tremendous results. From Alzheimer's to Yellow Fever medical science continues to unravel the mysteries of diseases ranging from symptomatic identification to medicinal procedures and pharmacological treatment.

The miracles of Western medicine are significant. Yet, because of these strides, we often overlook the limitations of the system. Reverence for one health care modality means we fail to recognize the profound healing capabilities of our own body. Reliance and focus on Western medicine as the only solution to health care issues becomes a disservice to our health as well as an economic burden on society.

What Hippocrates could not foresee was that increasing medical specialization would not keep the "whole patient" in mind. He certainly did not foresee the business implications of a philosophical trend. How is it, for example, that in the United States fifty million Americans do not have health insurance when approximately 17% of the GDP, two trillion dollars, goes toward healthcare? And, incredibly, instead of being amazingly healthy, 67% of Americans are overweight or obese, and 27% have blood pressure that is too high.

The viewpoint that permeates not only the medical establishment, but the general psyche, is that good health is NOT a natural state of being. Nor is the whole being as important as the specific body part or illness that needs attention. Instead, we have hundreds of thousands of discrete illnesses each representing a unique problem that can and should be solved. This PROBLEM and SOLUTION approach has been widely accepted because it supports a left brain, science oriented approach.

To some degree this approach is successful. You go to your doctor with your problem. He or she notes the symptoms. If there is not an obvious answer it is time for tests. Sometimes more tests. Perhaps a referral to other specialists, who are more familiar with your disease, the tests, or the symptoms. A cycle begins to narrow down the cause of your problem. When the problem is finally identified there is a high probability that the solution is going to be medicinal or pharmacological in nature.

Why not continue with this model? It does not take a rocket scientist, or a brain surgeon, to understand that this system has inherent flaws. Beyond unsustainable economics which have created a health care crisis in many countries, there are certain consequences for patients. The use of prescription drugs continues to skyrocket. Sales figures of drug companies, more than $30 billion annually, continue to rise in proportion to the money they spend to market prescription drugs directly to the public.

Physicians are influenced not only by drug companies, but also by consumers who come into the office knowing exactly what they need since they saw the advertisement on television. Even with the best abilities and intentions physicians rarely have time to work on more than the physical aspects of illness. By default they may ignore emotional, mental and spiritual aspects. In other words, *doctors and patients focus attention on the physical manifestation of what is ultimately an energetic disturbance.*

And, the discovery of a solution may not eliminate the illness. Like a cascading river, the discovery of one problem and its solution frequently leads to the discovery of a secondary problem that causes the first problem. Naturally, that has to be fixed. Symptomatic problems are being revealed, and hopefully solved.

This may be enough. However, if all the underlying issues that pertain to you as a specific individual are not fully addressed, then the problem, the illness, can return. Or, you develop a new problem. And the cycle starts over. The challenge for the medical establishment is that illness is initially diagnosed generically. In other words, there are a certain set of prescribed procedures to follow; that the patient also needs to follow. Further, it is impossible for the doctor(s) to both know and consider every aspect of your unique condition because in addition to the medicinal and physiological factors, there are a totally unique set of energetic conditions that have created *your* disease.

With modern medicine, the natural state of health, harmony and order, is not always established from inside the unique individual at a systemic level; but rather at the level of the symptoms and disease which may, or may not, be central to the condition.

Moving From the Physical to the Energetic

How can we then arrive at the perfect intersection of spirituality and modern medicine? Eastern systems have a different approach to moving patients toward a state of health. Instead of PROBLEM and SOLUTION, they consider human health, as nature itself, to be an ever evolving condition. Instead trying to solve a specific problem, they work on moving the entire patient to a natural state where health automatically returns to both the area that needs attention, and the entire body.

Let's consider four different viewpoints to better understand different methods of healing. One is the level of interaction. At this very basic level of interaction there is the molecular level of being. The language here is the physical body, which has become primarily the domain of physicians. As we move up one level we enter the realm of the mind. Words are the language of the mind; and the primary healing modality (in the West) resides with psychologists. Next we move up to the level of the soul. The soul responds to the language of images. A variety of healing modalities use images as the basis of healing. Meditation and visualization are examples. Finally, at the level of spirit, the language of interaction is energy itself. Shamans and energy healers work at this level.

Level of Interaction	The Language	Primary Healers
Spirit	Energy is the language	Shamans, energy healers
Soul	Images are the language	Meditation arts
Mind	Words are the language	Psychologists
Molecular	The physical body	Physicians

Alberto Villodo is a shaman, and the founder of The Four Winds Society. I meet him at a workshop entitled: *The Shamans Way of Healing, An introduction to Healing the Luminous Body*. He explains eloquently one of the differences between western medicine and shamanism. "We do not collude with the diagnosis. We do not treat cancer, multiple sclerosis, heart disease, etcetera. Rather, we bring energetic balance to the client. There is an energetic solution to every condition that comes in the door." Acknowledging that every tradition has merits, Alberto continues, "Western medicine is great for trauma. But it is not always good for chronic conditions. If you get bitten by a rattlesnake go immediately to the closest Emergency Room. The next day, go see your shaman to find out why the snake bit you."

Why Do We Get Out of Harmony?

What then are underlying issues for any specific disease for any one individual? Why do we even get sick? To answer this we have to take a step back from looking at any one disease or problem; and also a leap across a mental chasm in terms of understanding the nature of harmony and order. Forget any illness that you have had, currently have or will have. They are irrelevant. That is correct. The illness itself is irrelevant!

If we seek health not by fixing illness; but rather by understanding and moving towards a condition of harmony, we can achieve profound results for our unique set of circumstances. There are three primary reasons that harmony is disrupted. First, pre-conditioned patterns of habitual behavior. These encompass bad diets, lack of exercise and addictions. Major additions that affect health include alcohol, cigarettes and the multitude of illegal substances. Second, thoughts and emotions. What you think and feel directly creates conditions in your physical body. This relationship is often referred to as the mind-body connection. Third, stress and anxiety. Stress and anxiety can enter all areas of life. Relationships, career and finances and even health itself can all be affected by stress.

The leading cause of death in developed countries, cancer and heart disease, both stem from tension and stress. According to *Science Daily*: "New research has produced strong evidence of how work stress is linked to the biological mechanisms involved in the onset of heart disease."

But what exactly is stress? Stress is a physical and psychological response to excessive or prolonged demands that exceed our ability to cope. When you are stressed, or anxious, your mind becomes a problem producing factory. One problem leads to another. The repeated combination of mental, physical and psychological responses creates disharmony and illness.

Fight or Flight Creates Stress

The foundation of all stress comes from the "fight or flight" response that humans and animals have to stressful situations. It is in our individual and collective consciousness. Our DNA. A hungry Sabre Tooth Tiger chases you and your family up a tree. It is stressful. Kill the large cat, or run.

Thousands of years ago humans were more similar to other species in our biological tendencies. It was kill or be killed. Today, humans stand vastly apart from the 30 million other species which share Planet Earth. One of the major differences is how we react to stress.

All other species live their entire lives instinctually. Every action they perform is derived from built-in triggers. Pre-programmed responses for each species provide for their survival. The beauty of this system is that other species are forced to live in the moment. Your dog or cat doesn't sit around thinking, "Yesterday was such a bummer. My owners weren't home and I didn't get any treats or play time. But tomorrow… that will be different. Tomorrow is Saturday."

Animals live only in the present. Their response to stressful situations is as instantaneous as ours. But, and this is significant, after the cause of the stress is over, they are rapidly done with it. A hungry lion tears after a zebra. Both animals pump maximum adrenaline in a drama of real survival. The lion misses his catch as the zebra sweeps back into the herd. There is no after story. The lion does not linger on with self-pity and remorse thinking to himself, "I need to lose some weight. If I shed a few pounds I could catch that zebra."

Humans are a unique species. Free will gives us the power to create our own reality. We are not locked in step with all other humans as other animals are with their species. We are each individuals. The upside is that over the centuries we have used this individualism to create unique dreams and build human civilization. Using the vast power of our minds, we look backwards into our personal and collective history and forward into our future. We use this mental time-travel as a medium for analysis and for creation.

There is a downside. We also use our mind, our mental chatter, to bring us out of the present moment into Storyville. In Storyville stress can continue long after the event has occurred. Someone insults you, or disagrees with your opinion. It is not a Sabre Tooth Tiger, but you have your own personal fight or flight response. Leave the room or tell them to go to hell. The problem is that we do not stop. Long after the drama is over we are still in our head with it. "I should have said such and such. That would have put them in their place." Our body takes the story and partially or fully relives the stress-related response biologically. If this is not enough, we take Storyville into the future. "The next time I see so and so I will say such and such. Then they will understand where I am coming from." It is endless. We re-enact a stressful event that is already over, and project stressful events that probably won't happen. All the time our physical, emotional and mental bodies take a hit.

Use Intention to Step off the Merry-Go-Round

Imagine you are riding on a Merry-Go-Round and looking only at the other people on the ride. Everyone seems to be stationary. Possibly a few are going up and down on their horse. You do not see or feel that you are spinning. Just like we do not feel the rapid spinning of the Earth that creates gravity, and holds our feet to the ground. This is the challenge with stress. We only see or at acknowledge stress either at the time it occurs, or when health consequences arise. Even then we might not acknowledge the relationship between stress and a specific illness or physical condition. The first thing you have to do is let your analytical, left brain recognize the serious health consequences that come from your reactions to stress.

If you can acknowledge this relationship, that you are actually on a merry-go-round, then you can begin to make a shift.

Sankalpa is a Sanskrit word that means resolution, free will or determination. Medicine theory from India states that nature is the force that heals. Doctors and surgeons simply facilitate the process of natural healing. In order to achieve natural health you must access and use your innate healing powers. This is why individualized resolve, Sankalpa, is a basic tool in initiating the healing process. A well defined intention for your health creates the resolve for inner healing and allows nature to direct the process.

One of the best ways to stop any repetitive cycle that leads to stress is to go through the Intention setting process. Identify what causes you stress. Define the issues or stories that surround the stressor. Create an intention. Everyone will have a unique intention statement. Here are examples of intention statements that relate to health.

- I allow the love of my heart energy to dissolve physical, mental and emotional blocks stored in my body and mind as ill health, stress and tension.
- I allow the self-healing power of universal energy to restore harmony in my all aspects of my being.
- Every cell in my body radiates with the healing light of love that comes from within.
- I reside in complete harmony and peace with my inner self and my outer world.

Know Your Energy Body

Everything that exists is energy. The human body is one of the best examples of a highly evolved energy system. Philosophers, mystics and yogis describe the subtle, and not so subtle, energies of our natural environment and our own bodies. What is remarkable is that when dynamic energies converge in nature they form spinning circular patterns. Look at how a Category Five tornado with it's spinning energy twisting at three hundred miles per hour can lift a frame house off it's foundation.

Like nature, the human body has it's own subtle energy system. There are several words that describe the energy that runs through the body, including chi and prana. Both these translate as energy or life-force. We all have this life force energy; and how our life unfolds affects our life force energy.

The flow of prana through a network of power centers, paths and energy fields within and around the physical body are referred to as our energetic anatomy. Put more simply, our *energy body*. Some people call this your "aura." Whatever the terminology, your energy body is a three-dimensional field that moves from inside your physical body and emanates outward.

Chakra is a Sanskrit word, which translates as "wheel." Remember how shamans visualize nature to be defined by wheels. Chakras are considered to be power centers that both take in and distribute energy. Chakras are miniature versions of a hurricane. They are spinning energy centers. Your energetic anatomy contains three types of charkras.

> Major chakras 3 to 4 inches in diameter
> Minor chakras 1 to 2 inches in diameter
> Mini chakras less than 1 inch in diameter

Although most yogic texts refer to seven major chakras, there are actually 11 major chakras and innumerable smaller ones. You might envision chakra energy as emanating from the center of your body and moving outward. The following list provides the locations of the major chakras.

Crown -Top center of head
Forehead - In the center of your forehead
Anja - Between your eyebrows
Throat - At the middle of your throat
Heart - At the level of your heart, directly behind your sternum or breastbone
Back heart - Backside of your heart, on the spine between your shoulder blades
Front solar plexus - A few inches above your navel, below your sternum
Back solar plexus - Backside of the front solar plexus
Sacral - Slightly below navel
Sex - Behind the pubic bone
Basic - Base of spine

Chakras, these spirals of energy, differ in size and activity from one person to another. They can change based upon what is happening in your life physically, psychologically and spiritually. Chakras both take up and collect energy, and transform and pass on this energy. The unimpeded flow of energy through our body and our chakras determines our state of health, and mental and spiritual balance. Energy has an incredible intelligence and affinity to heal. One of the major blocks of the free flowing movement of energy is our mind. Specifically, our ego, which builds and holds onto stories that impede the flow of energy in the chakras.

Each chakra is associated with a physical area of the body, and often specific organs. Lower chakras are associated with fundamental emotions and basic survival needs. The finer energies and frequencies of the upper chakras correspond to higher mental and spiritual functions.

Crown (Sahasrara)
Location: Top of the head
Higher Self. Southwest position on a compass. Relates to the pituitary gland that controls the entire hormone system. Is associated with knowledge, understanding and connection to the universe. Energy moves into our body directly at this charka.

Brow (Ajna)
Location: Forehead
Ether Element. Southeast position on a compass. Above the center of the eyes and inside the head. Linked to the pineal gland related to activity and rest and directs our intuition and imagination. Ether, space and hearing. INFINITY as mantra.

Throat (Vishuddha)
Location: Throat
Air Element. Center of a compass. Tied into thyroid gland, related to our metabolic rate and mineral levels. It manifests communication.

Heart (Anahata)
Location: Center of chest
Relationships. North position on a compass. Relates to the thymus gland for growth and immune systems. Directly related to love and relationships. HARMONY as mantra.

Solar Plexus (Manipura)

Location: Just above naval

Fire Element. South position on a compass. Ties to the complex of nerves connected here and touches adrenal glands and pancreas. Relates to personal energy. It is a major area for holding anxiety and issues. This area of our body transforms food into nutrients and waste. Contentment is a mantra.

Sacral (Svadistana)

Location: Slightly below naval

Water Element. West position on a compass. It is associated with our creativity, emotions, sensuality and reproduction.

Base (Muladhara)

Location: Base of spine

Earth Element. East position on compass. Located at the base of our spine, it grounds us and impacts our personal survival instinct. Our sense of smell is connected to the earth.

Chakras and Health

One chakra is not better than another. They are equally significant and all play a role in our physical, emotional, mental and spiritual health. The energy of your chakras is constantly in motion. Your chakra energy is different today than it was yesterday. Different now than an hour ago. In terms of health, your physical body can perform at optimum health when all of your chakras are balanced and energized. Energy moves freely both horizontally, in and out from each chakra, and vertically, up and down through your body.

Mental and physical disease is caused by a blockage of energy. Balancing the chakras, working with the energy of the chakras, is one way to maintain health. It also prevents you from getting stuck in the repetitive stories that create stress, disharmony and illness.

There is another aspect of chakras that is significant. You move your body all day long. You EXPERIENCE things horizontally. But you LEARN things vertically as the energy of an experience moves through all of your chakras. This is another reason to keep chakras opened and balanced. You learn better.

Notice, for example, how the second chakra, the sacral, is identified as the chakra of water. The seat of emotions and reproduction. Here, and in the solar plexus, is where emotions and transformative energies focus and move. When you experience a strong emotion it is not uncommon to literally feel the physical impact of the emotion in the area of your body where the Solar Plexus is located. This is undoubtedly where the expression "I have a gut feeling" comes from.

Exercise, Muscles and Prana

We engage in exercise because it makes us feel good. Exercise balances and energizes chakras. Right after a good workout you can feel the energy flowing in your body. Your mind is bright and you feel alive. Your body is a fantastic vehicle to help you ground into the present moment. Your muscles provide one gateway to your energy body. Your body contains 650-odd muscles that make up almost half your total body weight. The biggest one is your gluteus maximus. The use of muscle opens the channels of your subtle energy, which balances the chakras.

I participate in a ten day, silent retreat with yoga teacher Sarah Powers. I do not know it is a silent retreat until the first evening. Sarah says, "This is a silent retreat. If there is there anyone here who did not know this, you can raise your hand." After a quick scan of the room I see no hands are raised. I have a fast conversation with myself and decide it is better to simply start being quiet right now. What can possible go wrong?

Sarah is as vibrant as she is flexible. She has a beautiful smile that says, "You too can stretch like this and have fun." Sarah teaches a combination of Yin (passive) and Yang (active) yoga. Yin yoga is when you passively hold a pose for a longer than normal period of time. We sit in Gomukasana. Translated as "cow face pose", it is a pose where you fold your legs over on top of each other. One knee directly above the other. You feel the stretch immediately. We fold over, let our heads drop down and rest on our legs. Then sit. For fifteen minutes.

Because it opens the deep connective tissues that surround your joints, Yin Yoga allows energy to move into places that are normally stagnant, even during exercise. It also opens the energetic pathways of the meridian system. Prana stimulates and tones your joints and these deep connective tissues as energy blocks are removed. A flood of prana into previously clogged areas improves your nervous system. You become calm and focused, which helps tremendously if you want to remain silent and present.

When you exercise it is the opening of your subtle energy body that creates euphoria. You ignite the subtle energy body by activating muscles at their core. Once prana flows freely you can learn how to move and respond to life based upon the natural direction and intuition that prana provides.

How to Balance and Energize Your Chakras

Massage therapists open your muscles to release toxins and balance your chakras. They energetically and physically adjust and open your body to help energy move freely. Aromatherapy and smudging can clear and balance chakras. Crystal bowls, Tibetan singing bowls, gongs and didgeridoo all produce sounds and tones that stream into your body and open your chakras for healing, balancing and meditation. This is also true of mantras. The power of mantra is in the healing aspect of the sound which goes directly into your body. You can see by these examples that the energy of your chakras can be balanced by using a variety of techniques. Exercise, massage, sound. They use energy to move energy.

It is important to balance your chakras before you energize them. Balancing, cleaning and purification of chakras opens them up so your physical body can be receptive to spiritual energy. Imagine your body has a water hose that runs down your spine. If any part of the hose is blocked the water is not going to move through. It is going to get stuck somewhere. The entire hose, all the chakras, need to be clean before you turn on the water.

What can you do when you are sitting in front of a computer screen, or riding the subway, and you know that your energy is not balanced? You don't have a Tibetan singing bowl handy and your massage isn't scheduled for another week. Fortunately, there is one energy process that you have access to all the time. **This is your breath.**

Your breath represents a miraculous system. Of all the bodily functions we have, breathing is the most important. Think about it. You can survive without food for as long as four weeks. You can survive without water for four to ten days. But you die within three minutes if you can't breath. Further, breathing is the only system that is part of the autonomic nervous system AND under our direct control. The autonomic nervous system controls blood pressure, heart and breathing rates, body temperature, digestion, metabolism, the balance of water and electrolytes and the production of body fluids.

You do not have to think to breath. In the middle of the night your body is going to continue to breathe without asking permission. You can also control your breathing. You can change the rate of your breathing. You can breathe deeply or shallowly. You can breathe in one nostril and out the other. You can hold your breath.

Your Breath Can Balance Your Chakras

All of creation is a manifestation of the interaction of polarity. The interaction of yin and yang, male and female. Every person has male and female attributes. The unification of the positive and negative elements within us, the male and female, creates balance. That is why the practice of Hatha Yoga is designed to bring balance between these two forces within your body. **HA** refers to the right nostril; and **THA** refers to the left nostril.

For thousands of years yogis have studied, experimented and learned how to use breath as a medium to balance chakras and steady the mental fluctuations of our mind. Indeed, the purpose of all forms and aspects of yoga is to quiet the fluctuations of your mind. This harmonizes mind, body and spirit. Your own breath can be a vehicle for this harmony in the system of pranayama. Remember, prana means energy, and *ayama* means control. Pranayama is the control of energy with breathing.

In addition to life supporting oxygen, with each breath in you absorb all of the positive energy of the Air Element. This energy can be used to clean, balance and energize your chakras. The vital energy and oxygen move not only into your lungs; but rapidly reach the blood, organs, tissues, nerves and cells.

It is not a mistake that you have two nostrils. The breath that moves through your right nostril represents the Sun. The right nostril breath connects with the left side of your brain. The breath that moves through your left nostril represents the Moon. The breathing of your left nostril connects with the right side of your brain.

Running down the center of your spine is an energy channel known as the Sushumna. Starting at the base of your spine and snaking up around this central channel are two side channels. These channels, called the Ida Nadi and Pingala Nadi, intersect and cross each other at every chakra all the way up to the Ajna chakra, your Third Eye.

The ida nadi represents the feminine, ying energy of your body. It carries cooling, meditative, feminine energy. The ida nadi ends in your left nostril. The pingala nadi represents the masculine, yang energy of your body. It carries warming, active, masculine energy and ends in your right nostril.

You can open and balance your chakras when energy flows through the sushumna. This occurs when ida and pingala are in balance. As prana flows through the sushumna it activates each chakra. This helps bring energy and health to that physical area of the body, and the organs connected to the chakra. It also brings balance to the emotions related to each chakra. In this state of balance you can achieve meditative awareness.

Alternate nostril breathing is one way to bring balance into your breath and harmony to your chakras, mind, body and spirit. It connects and energizes the two hemispheres of your brain. This balance extends to your chakras. It calms your mind. It allows energy to move freely through your body, which empowers your body to use it's natural healing abilities.

You may notice that when you are in a state of balance and harmony it is reflected in your breathing. You are in balance when your breath is calm, steady and flows easily. You are out of balance when your breathing is uneven, rapid or congested. The many moods that you have during the course of a day are reflected and connected to the variations in your breathing patterns.

The Science of Breathing

There are four essential elements to every breath you take. You inhale, then hold or pause, exhale, then hold or pause and begin again.

Inhalation	Puraka
Pause	Kumbhaka
Exhalation	Rechaka
Pause	Kumbhaka

Normally we only think "in and out." The pauses are also important. When you take air in and hold it, the retention period is the time when oxygen gets absorbed into your bloodstream. The pause in your breath becomes a moment when you get close to being absolutely still.

The pause can increase your ability to concentrate. It can also strengthen your understanding and control over your life. Extremely practiced yogis maintain the retention period for upwards of five minutes. All the rhythmic cycles of the universe are composed of these same movements. The universe itself expands, pauses, contracts and expands again. Of course it takes a little longer. Right now our galaxy, the Milky Way, is in the final stage of it's expansion.

What is amazing is that you can consciously change the pattern of your breath at any time to change your mental state. The Breath Chart shows a few variations of breathing. You can do these variations with both of your nostrils open, breathing through the nose. You can also do them as alternate nostril breathing. Hold one nostril closed while you inhale through the other nostril. Hold the air in. Close the other nostril and exhale. Hold out. Repeat by inhaling now with the nostril that is open, and which you did not inhale with the first time. This opens the ida and pingala channels. The numbers are "counts." If you have a medical condition you should consult your physician before doing anything new.

Inhale	Hold	Exhale	Hold	Results
2	8	4	8	Relax
6	3	6	3	Balance
6	6	6	1	Energize

Breathing and Consciousness

There is a direct connection between breathing and our physical, mental and emotional state. There is something else. Breathing is consciousness. When you breathe you carry more than nourishing energy into your body. Consciousness itself can ride on your breath as easily as a surfer can ride on waves of water. This is important. With every breath you take in you can impart your intention onto your breath. Here is a simple self-guided exercise that combines the power of breath, visualization, intention and full chakra balancing.

EXERCISE

Balance Your Chakras

Sit in a comfortable position. Close your eyes and consciously slow down your breathing. Be aware of your crown chakra, the very center of the top of your head, and above this area. Visualize golden light, the color of morning sunlight. This magnificent color has been imprinted on you since the day you were born. Imagine a stream of golden sunlight moving down into your body through your crown chakra. It flows into your head, back through the center of your head to the back of your head and then down your spine. As you breathe in carry in life, vitality, energy and love. Let your intention ride in on the in-breath. When the golden light reaches the base of your spine release the energy and begin your exhalation. Let your breath and the golden light flow up the front of your body, out your arms and also back up through your throat and again out the top of your head. Release the energy. On your out-breath exhale negativity, emotions, what you no longer need. If you do this slowly, consciously, you may feel the energy moving in your body. This exercise can be done for just a few minutes, or it can be used to guide you into a deeper state of relaxation and meditation.

Depression and Mental Health Issues

According to research studies as many as twenty-six percent of adults may suffer from a mental disorder in any one year.[1] Globally, hundreds of millions of people experience something ranging from mood swings and mild depression to major depression, anxiety disorder, panic disorder, obsessive compulsive disorder, bipolar disorder, post traumatic stress disorder (PSTD), social phobia, eating disorder, attention deficit hyperactivity disorder (ADHD), autism, dysthymic disorder, alzemheimer's and suicide.

These are serious problems. Look at how many of these mental problems have the word "disorder" as part of their label. Clearly things are not in order. What is out of order is energetic balance. There are hundreds of individual disorders, and millions of individual people. There is not a generic diagnosis for all of us. Each person is totally unique. Consult your physician before you do anything new.

Modern society has overcome many issues related to physical hunger. We have replaced them with mental issues. In my yoga and energy workshops people write down issues they are dealing with. Visit my web site **ThriveInside.Net** if you would like to schedule a workshop. Common sharing includes:

> *"I have low self esteem, self doubt and depression."*
> *"I do not believe in myself, and often think that I am not good enough."*
> *"I do not accomplish enough with my life."*
> *"I am not worthy of great success or wealth."*

People are surprised when they hear the person next to them voice what is on their mind. These are common problems. Ironically, these mental issues are not dissimilar from survival issues surrounding not having enough food. These are basic survival issues that often have roots in the first chakra (Basic) and the third charka (Solar Plexus).

Self-sabotaging thoughts create energetic seeds of failure, disease and depression. Thought forms are extremely powerful. They create self-fulfilling prophesies; and they can make us feel bad about ourselves. It is a

---

1 Kessler RC, Chiu WT, Demler O, Walters EE. Prevalence, severity, and comorbidity of twelve-month DSM-IV disorders in the National Comorbidity Survey Replication (NCS-R). Archives of General Psychiatry, 2005 Jun;62(6):617-27.

downward spiral. In fact, when you experience a mental disorder it can be difficult to recognize the space you are in because you are absorbed with it. There are an infinite number of reasons that we acquire these thought forms. Everything from artificial pressures we place on ourselves to news we digest to energetic projections from family and colleagues.

There is a lot of negative mojo that needs to be cleaned. One of the big challenges with energy is that most of us can't see it. If we are lucky we can feel it. Consider how most people react when their car gets covered with mud. They are at the car wash the same day. We are obsessed with keeping the physical objects that surround our life perfectly clean. We take a shower every day. We wash the dishes. Clean the windows. It only makes sense that we would want our energy body to be clean. I know more mental problems are caused by an energetic imbalance than by a lack of sanitation.

There are two paths to consider. One is the quick fix. This is when you enter an unhealthy mental space and you recognize that you don't want to be there. Use whatever tools and techniques you find in this book that help you achieve energetic balance. Breath work, aromatherapy, grounding, smudging. Do what works for you.

The second path is more permanent. It involves a regular practice of energetic balancing and cleaning. Yoga Nidra, meditation, exercise, dietary considerations, pranic healing. The key is consistency. Like taking a shower or washing the car. It is consistent practice that creates an enduring energetic space. Negative thought forms begin to wash away. Increasingly they have a hard time finding a foothold in which to take root.

Use Your Heart Center to Connect to Source

The average human heart pumps some 6,000 quarts of blood a day. That is 1,500 gallons of life giving plasma that move through your body daily. This makes drinking the recommended dose of eight glasses of water a day seem like nothing. In addition to being a miraculous workhorse, the heart represents love. It always has. From the heart shape in Valentine's Day boxes of chocolate back to Egyptian mythology, the heart symbolizes how we energetically relate to other people, and to ourselves.

The Heart Chakra, Anahata, relates directly to the physical thymus gland which is a center for growth and immune systems. Therefore, the heart is a natural healer because the heart chakra corresponds to the immune system. It also relates to love. This powerful combination of physiological and emotional healing can bring accord to all aspects of your being. Specifically, the heart chakra can instantaneously transmute any emotion or energy into a state of non-reactive harmony. In relationships this is good for you; and for the people you are with.

You do not want to bottle up anger, resentment or other emotional energies. If you do and they are not released they find their way into your physical body. And, not just into your brain cells. Like remnants of a cheeseburger that you ate in high school; unresolved emotional energies get stored, tightly lodged in areas of your physical body. Commonly it is in the hip area. It is one reason that many yoga postures focus on hip opening as a form of release.

Here is what you do. The moment you find yourself in reaction to any event, person or circumstance, move to non-reactive awareness. This is challenging because you have to be conscious of your desire to have an emotional reaction before you have it. Catch yourself. If the reaction is related to a conversation you are having with someone you can put a quick stop to the confrontational energy that is spiraling upwards.

If negative verbal energy is directed towards you, focus on your Ajna chakra between your eyebrows and say to yourself, "Dissolve. Dissolve." This dissipates the energy before it can move and attach to your other chakras. You can also help the other person disintegrate their energy. Simply say, "I hear what you are saying." If the topic is really more about their issue than yours say, "I totally agree with you." It is what the other person needs to hear. Let them hear it and dissolve the emotional charge of the moment. If you know that you cannot handle your own emotional reaction say, "I am sorry but I have to leave now. Perhaps we can continue this conversation tomorrow."

Immediately use the amazing capability of your own heart chakra to transmute the emotional energy into positive love for yourself and for the other. Focus on your heart charka and allow it to dissolve the energy inside you. If you want to help the other person, visualize loving energy streaming from your heart chakra to the other person. This will help put out the emotional fire that is brewing. You need to quickly bless and forgive the other person. Never harbor anger. The reason to do this is as much for you as for them. Your reaction to the other person is what will come back to you.

EXERCISE

Allow Your Heart Chakra to Open Forgiveness and Love

If you are unable to transmute the energy and the situation at the time; you can still help yourself and the other person later. Your heart chakra energy grows stronger if you energize it. Sit in a calm and comfortable position and place the palm of your left hand over your heart; and place the palm of your right hand over your left. Your palms contain chakras that boost the energy that moves into your heart chakra. As you breathe in, let the energy move from behind your body back through your heart center and out the front of your body to infinity. As you exhale, allow healing energy to move back in through your hands deep into your heart center. It is like a slow moving wave. Your palm chakras enhance the energy in this ebb and flow, elevating the ability of your heart chakra to transmute energy. Continue, and allow your heart chakra to open and expand. You can even use this as a meditation without thought. Listen to your breathing; feel the energy flow and your heart chakra open.

In this state of awareness you can forgive yourself and the other person for the interaction. Erase it completely. Allow the energy of the interaction to dissolve for both of you. As your heart chakra dissolves and heals the negative energy it also erases the story that created it. Prevent the event and the story from becoming an imprint that you will live again.

There is a proverb: Time Heals All Wounds. More accurately time fades the story of emotional wounds. It does not mean the story has been erased; only moved to a back shelf. When another event comes by that is similar to the event that caused the wound your reactions will be the same; and the wound can appear again even when there is no need for it. It is important to dissolve any negative energy and the story surrounding the energy. If you have an old emotional wound you can use this process to help dissolve it. You don't need to make a big project out of it. The goal is not to relive every bad experience you've had. But when emotions come up as a reaction to events, memories, or feelings, you can use your heart chakra as a vehicle for transmutation to send love and forgiveness to yourself and the others involved.

This can work in mysterious ways. The universe does not acknowledge time and space the way our brains do. Time and space are irrelevant to the universe. For example, perhaps you have lost a loved one. You always wish that you had said or done something different for that person before they passed. Open your heart chakra with your palms. Give that gift to them and yourself right now. You will notice a difference in the way you feel.

The Relationship of Disease and Story

Cheyenne Maloney has beautiful grey hair that streams down both sides of a face sculptured like a Greek Goddess. From the moment you meet her, she takes you off guard. Her gaze is soft and gentle; yet she looks right through you. A shaman of the highest order, Cheyenne has, through personal experience and training, acquired the ability to fully embrace the unity of all existence. In plain English this means she knows who you are before you do.

I first meet Cheyenne in a Circle. Twenty people sit in this circle with Cheyenne. She is talking about stories. Her own story and the stories we create. "Know," she says, "the capsule you have created as yourself. Be aware of it as an imagined reality. Awareness rises into a field. Right now you could be a socialite or a wino. Both are real possibilities right now!"

I know exactly what she means. Not just the words, but the truth of it. That, like a blanket, stories of a lifetime with all their hidden agendas, can be pulled off of us as easily as a layer of clothing.

Cheyenne continues to share a critical aspect of her teachings which are the foundation of phenomenal healing. She believes the dramas and dreams that fuel our motivations are most often solidified during childhood. That there may have been one or more experiences that moved us from a state of innocence and connection to source, to a place where stories created and solidified by our ego, begin to have power over our life and health. Whether those experiences were traumatic or incidental, they have lasting impact. In the arena of health, what happens is the creation of a story about sickness. Specifically, "this sickness is me... this sickness is not me."

What happens is that our lens of perception is unequivocally altered. The shamanic term for this lens is Assemblage Point. The term carries more significance and depth than simply thinking it is our "world view" or "belief system." In his book *The Art of Dreaming*, Carlos Castaneda discusses teachings given by a Yaqui sorcerer and shaman he refers to as "don Juan."

Don Juan describes the assemblage point as a visible vortex of energy. This energy body creates a luminous egg, an auric field, that surrounds each of us. Most important, according to don Juan, is the location of the point where this egg is formed - the assemblage point. It is described as being about two and a half feet behind and above our right shoulder blade. Don Juan explains that the position of the assemblage point determines our perception of the world, and how we feel and behave. Because most humans have a similar assemblage point, we see and experience the world in relatively the same manner.

Looking across the room of students, but seemingly directly at me with an intensity that showers me with sincerity and urgency, Cheyenne adds, "Every second we recreate ourselves. Our identity *and* our destiny. This is about waking up from your life."

This is a critical. It is easy to misinterpret the concept of "waking up" as something that we have to do, or add to our life. In reality, it is about taking away from what we have already layered on. When all of the stories are stripped away the only thing that remains is who you really are.

The second aspect of Cheyenne's work is to energetically re-align the assemblage point. For Cheyenne the assemblage point is a band of energy that runs, when it is balanced and aligned, directly through the heart chakra. More than simply the Heart Chakra, it is anchored at the depth of the heart. Located at the core of our heart and being.

Cheyenne energetically determines if the assemblage point has shifted away from its true alignment. Then, using an incredibly large quartz crystal and a process of energetic movement, the band of energy, the assemblage point, is carefully realigned to a place where optimum perception and health can occur naturally.

I have had two Shifts. Both times I felt energy moving inside my body even though I was sitting very comfortably in a chair. I felt what I can only describe as an activation of my heart center. A tugging right in the middle of my chest. Afterwards, incredible peace.

Truly, perception is altered. The most powerful perceptual change after the shift was that when I look at other people I can see past their mask, beyond their stories, to who they are. We sat in Circle after one shift. I was sitting across from a middle aged woman. She was overweight and holding an oxygen tank because she had breathing problems that seemed like they came from smoking cigarettes. Normally I would look at her situation and create compassion in my mind. After the Shift, I could see the smile in her eyes. She was so happy. I never would have seen this. To look and see what is really there instead of a story that your mind creates. Even something as valuable as compassion can be built on a false story. The German poet Johann Wolfgang von Goethe echos this when he wrote: "What is the most difficult of all things? What seems to you to be the easiest: to see with your eyes what your eyes are looking at."

The Story is Intertwined with the Energy

There is a paradox. On the one hand there is a direct relationship between any illness you have and your stories about yourself. And, on the other hand, the energy does not care about the stories. These two truths can be powerful as complimentary therapies that don't involve drugs or surgery.

Let's start with the story. Sometimes we can have and hold onto a disease or illness because it serves a psychological need. One way that illness serves us is with attention. We receive attention from others when we are ill. That is a good thing. To a point. It no longer serves our health if the illness lingers on past the point of normal recovery. You might think that nobody wants to be sick any longer than they have to. Logically, that is true. But the mysteries of the mind and ego are complicated.

The attention we receive might not even be from other people. You might be the only person who is really giving a lot of attention to your own medical problem. It might be a hangnail or toe fungus. Still, on some level, the illness may serve a purpose. Ask yourself if there is any possible connection between the illness and the attention that it receives? If you feel there is, then you can create an intention to work with this issue.

Now consider a more serious medical problem than a hangnail. Asthma, heart disease, liver failure ....you name it. The disease has a specific relationship with the individual who is having the problem. This cannot be denied. The only question is whether the relationship is purely medicinal. It is both convenient and habitual to use the perceptual lens of western science to understand disease. Diabetes, heart disease, Alzheimer's. In the world of medical science we have DNA markers, and hereditary influences. Our parents, uncles, grandfathers had a certain disease so we have a predisposition to it. That is one viewpoint. Another viewpoint, perhaps with a different assemblage point, considers energetic healing and spontaneous recovery.

Can disease survive when the person it is sticking to no longer exists? Can it survive when their environment completely disappears? If you are dead your disease will not hang around much longer. But what if you simply became a different person? All of your stories about yourself suddenly disappear. Not just your "belief system" but the essence of your acquired personality. Could this create an environment within your physical body that would disassociate itself from the disease? In Cheyenne's world it could.

It is a challenge to understand healing at this level. First, the connection between the physical and energetic worlds is not obvious. Second, when you have a physically illness the symptoms can be so profound that you simply want them to disappear. You have a better chance of faster recovery, and smaller chance of reoccurrence, if you can associate and then disassociate a physical condition with its energetic foundation. Shamans and energy healers clear imprints by working through the chakras, which are the interface to the body's luminous energy field. At this level, you do not need to identify stories to heal. Healing becomes a journey; not an intervention.

SAFARI: Locate and Seal Up Your Energy Sink Holes

A safari is a journey. In the ongoing journey of our own life we encounter numerous experiences. The experiences are all learning opportunities.

We only get into problems when we take our reactions from a previous experience, and layer that on top of what is happening at this moment. We incorrectly color this moment with our previous experience. Then our energy body, our prana, can not flow properly. Instead of moving in response to what is happening, it gets blocked and diverted with the mental projections we bring from the past.

Beauty is in the eyes of the beholder; and so are problems. Restore your relationship with yourself. Restore the balance between your extremely mental left brain and your intuitive right brain. Restore harmony in your body. Restore your connection to source.

Like nature, our body wants to be in a state of harmony. It wants to heal. There are five patterns that can scatter precious energy. When your energy is diverted you feel tired, or become prone to illness. Like a leaky hose, all of the energy seeps out through cracks we don't even know exist. As you become conscious of the ways in which you leak energy, you can catch yourself, contain and re-direct that energy for useful purposes. You can prevent energetic imprints from being activated. Being present in life is not only about enjoying every moment; it is also about conserving your energy in such a way that the present moment automatically becomes the pinnacle of your consciousness.

S-A-F-A-R-I

1. Self Image
There is a desire to have every situation assist in the reinforcement of our self image. It takes energy to re-craft the story of the moment in order to see yourself in a certain light. Recognize it and give it up.

2. Assumptions
We assume that we understand a situation. But our viewpoint may not accurately reflect the present situation. We base our analysis on past experiences that we consider to be identical situations.

3. Fractured Mind
The fractured mind occurs when we think about multiple things. We are not present in the moment; but instead are using our mind to think and listen to our own thoughts. With the invention of computers we have created the concept of "multi-tasking." A PDA can simultaneously make a phone call, calculate an equation, sort photos and play games. Actually,

your computer can do these things simultaneously. Your brain can not. We believe we are multi-tasking because our mind moves quickly. You can drive, talk on a cell phone and listen to music. It seems like it is all happening at the same time. But your brain is simply moving from A to B to C back to A in rapid sequence. Your brain can only do one thing at a time. When we emulate a computer, rapidly moving from one conscious thought to another, it requires energy. The more rapidly we shift, the more scattered our energy. The result has been referred to as *continuous partial attention*. We are not fully present.

4. Addictions

Addictions are something we like to do again, and again. There can be a physical component to an addiction that involves a drug, such as alcohol or nicotine. But there is also a story. A desire to re-create a story, an experience that we have had and find pleasurable. Or, a desire to escape the story we are currently living. Did you ever wonder why alcohol is also referred to as Spirits? Because your spirit literally moves outside your physical body. If you go to a wild party some people don't seem to be in their body. Their spirit has decided to move away from the currently uninhabitable physical form. Regardless of the cause, additions require significant energy, and take us out of the present moment.

5. Reaction

Reactions occur when we don't accept what is happening. Being impatient in a long line. Feeling too hot on a summer afternoon. We often react to our own reaction. Being upset makes us more upset. We need to find Beginner's Mind to see other people, especially people that we've known for a long time as both new and as now. Not as they were before.

6. Inappropriate Emotions

In one sense emotions are never inappropriate. They represent an expression and a release of feelings. What can become unhealthy is when emotions take on a life of their own that has no relationship to what is happening now. Instead of reacting to the current situation, you are reacting to other events and bringing those reactions to bear on this moment. We bottle up the previous emotional release and hold it hostage. Not only can this confuse the person who is the recipient of the current melt down; but it also puts an energy signature on the current event. In other words the current moment is not only incorrectly viewed, but it is now labeled with the emotional release of the other experience.

I do not suggest you walk around all day critiquing your use of energy in all these scenarios. That would drive you crazy. Rather, work on creating a sense of self awareness. Be in touch with who you truly are and what is actually happening. In terms of health, when you begin to make simply adjustments to your use of energy in these situations you not only have more energy; you will also allow your energy to automatically redirect for self healing.

The Nature of Miracles

Health and miracles seem to go together like vanilla ice cream and chocolate syrup. There are several reasons for this. When we get a disease, or our physical health deteriorates beyond the point where traditional medicine can play a role, it seems appropriate to call in the assistance of a higher power. If modern medicine, with it's bag of miracles (Penicillin, insulin, etc.), can't get the job done, then we either look for, or surrender, to forces beyond the normal state of affairs.

All religions recognize that miracles have been performed by certain individuals. Muhammad, Jesus, Buddha and Moses all performed miracles with capabilities that arose through divine assistance. While miracles come in many different forms, and for many different purposes; dealing with illness and disease is a common area. What is more personal than our own health or the health of relatives or loved ones? What is more powerful than a cure that comes outside of the realm of traditional medicine?

Miracles are usually not viewed as being performed by an individual, but rather *through* an individual. The individual only channels the miracle. It is one reason that many people pray to saints and great masters after their death. Since their soul does not die upon physical death they can intervene on your behalf after they have passed.

One hot Sunday in June I stand in the back of the cavernous, white walled congregation room of the majestic Church of San Francisco in Antigua, Guatemala. A service is in session and rows of wooden pews are filled to capacity. The audience is largely Guatemalan. Wearing the colorful robes of their culture, the room vibrates with an energy that comes from both devoted attention and brilliant fabrics. An intuitive understanding suddenly rushes through my body. I feel that God is looking directly out of the eyes of all these people. God is living through them as much as being part of them. It is a feeling I shall never forget.

The Church of San Francisco continues to honor Santo Hermano Pedro de San Jose de Betancourt, or simply Hermano Pedro. Brother Pedro was born in the Canary Islands. He arrived in Antigua, Guatemala on February 18, 1651. In his lifetime brother Pedro helped the poor and the sick. He left a legacy of miracles performed during and after his lifetime. His remains lie in the church. Because of the example set by him in his life, as well as the miracles attributed to him, Pope John Paul II beatified him on June 22, 1980, in St. Peter's Basilica, in Rome. On July 30, 2002, the Pope canonized him during his third trip to Guatemala. Brother Pedro became Guatemala's first Saint.

Later that day I return to pray and give my respects in silent reverence in a small chamber off the main room. Beside me is a large wooden wall filled from bottom to top with a cacophony of little photographs, notes, jewelry and wooden crutches. Many are prayers for assistance needed; many others are thanks for assistance provided.

The Recipe for Miracles

Who would not want a healing miracle? If colleges could offer degrees in miracles attendance would skyrocket. What really is behind the nature of a miracle? When we get extremely sick and have a rapid or unexpected recovery we may call it a Miracle. Miracles happen every moment. We are miracles. Our viewpoint distorts this simple truth. Since we live most of the time in a state of good health, it becomes the norm. We expect it. But this is the miracle. Just opening our eyes in the morning and pulling in breath that starts the day is a miracle. Our bodies are designed to heal and survive in amazing ways.

I am sitting in a large hotel ballroom in Saint Louis listening to Grand Master Choa Kok Sui, founder of modern Pranic Healing. It is now four years after that first workshop with his disciple Master Stephen Co. I study regularly with this system. Today I am excited not only to be in the presences of such a master, but also because we are learning how to see auras. I have no expectations. I have only seen what I consider to be an aura one time. It was after meditating with a guru and a small group of his disciples on the floor of his living room. When we finished the meditation I slowly opened my eyes and looked at the guru and the woman sitting beside him. They both had golden light moving around their shoulders and above their head. And now, although I use energy for healing, I have never seen the rainbow-like colors that are shown in illustrations of auras and chakras.

Grand Master Choa finishes his detailed instructions for the group. He asks for a participant to come onto the stage. A young man jumps up. The entire room practices the procedures as Grand Master Choa moves over to the young man. He gently places his hand onto the young mans shoulder. Instantly I see a series of rainbow like colors, all in ribbons, one on top of the other, appear around the young man. I practically stop breathing.

It is an awesome experience to visually see the energy field of a human being. For me, the experience of seeing an aura is on par with what I would term a miracle. Because this was the last I met Master Choa before his passing it became a special memory filled with love and admiration.

Does this mean that every person can use laws of nature and access divine intelligence and perform what may be considered a miracle? Absolutely. Will we all perform miracles? No. Does it diminish the stature of great masters like Muhammad, Jesus or Buddha to state that we all have the innate ability to perform miracles? No. It honors them.

It is clear that great religious founders and leaders give themselves entirely to a higher purpose. Their intense devotion and sacrifice open doors to a rare understanding of the human condition and universal principals. These enlightened souls could have no greater joy or no higher honor than when any living person taps into and expresses the same wisdom that they share. In other words, by entering a state where miracles occur, it is possible to simultaneously perform unique feats, but also honor the lineages and individuals who show us the way.

Swami Sri Kripalvanandji, known more widely as Swami Kripalu or Babuji, asked his guru Dadaji an important question, "How does a yogi become enlightened?" The response was straightforward: "When the disciple of the disciple becomes enlightened."

Healing and Dying

Each person responds to a different method of healing. For some, a pharmaceutical will do the job perfectly. For others, acupuncture provides better results. My suggestion is that if you are not getting results that satisfy you, consider trying a different modality. Know that miracles happen.

Know that sickness is a messenger that tells you about your life and yourself. Know, without bowing down to any false story of illness, that illness and dying are acceptable outcomes. Each of us will be ready to die at a different time, under different circumstances. It is not the job of any healer to determine what that time should be. It is the job of a healer to help a person heal; and healing *can* result in death. Healing is successful when, even in the course of dying, we make our way back home consciously.

Notes and Experiences

NATURE'S DIVINE GIFTS 3

My head throbs, my muscles are sore, and I can't breathe. I would like to lie on the couch and look out my window. A sea of trees cascade down into a lush green valley that sits in front of snow capped mountains. Ravens and hawks circle gracefully on ever changing thermals. But I must leave to see Amma Sri Karunamayi. She is visiting Denver and will give a darshan, a lecture, and bless every person who attends individually. I don't know much about Amma. A few close friends have studied with her for many years and strongly recommend that I make a connection.

I muster the energy required to drive down to the city. It's about an hour drive. It is July and the sun is shinning through a sky that seems unnaturally blue. As I enter the church I notice that Amma's followers have set up a store in the lobby with literally hundreds of books, cds, figurines, rosaries and prints. In fact, there are so many things available that I suddenly realize that Amma is quite prolific in sharing her teachings.

The church is large and seats five hundred. Arriving late I move to the pews on the left side of the room because I can get a little closer to the front of the room. I always feel better when I get physically close to my teachers. It seems that I can energetically as well as mentally pick up on their teachings.

After a brief introduction by an assistant, Amma jumps into discourse. I am surprised as she begins to share the latest research in bio-psychology. How our disconnection with nature has inadvertently changed our brain chemistry through everything from pesticides to fertilizers to genetic engineering. And these illnesses that we have created for ourselves pull us away from understanding and experiencing our divine nature and the gifts of nature. She says, "Mother Nature gives so much to you, sunlight, water, vital energy. If anyone loves Mother Nature, that person will become wise."

As she continues to share I realize that I don't feel very well. In fact I need to lie down. There's no one sitting on my left so I slouch over. I don't want to be disrespectful so I keep my feet on the ground. After an hour Amma begins to wrap up her presentation. She is beaming as she declares, "I love you millions and millions of times, I love you billions and billions of times. I love you zillions and zillions of times. I love you trillions and trillions of times. I love you countless gazillions of times."

Now it is time for individual blessings. Amma allows every person in the audience to come up and speak directly with her about any issue in their life. And she offers her blessings. People begin to form orderly lines and walk up for their time with Amma. As people move toward Amma I can feel their excitement and devotion. In fact, this is bi-directional devotion. Amma sits with a glorious smile expectantly waiting for time with each person. I realize that while I am near the front of the room that they are actually moving this snake-like procession around in such a way that my little pew will be one of the last to be called. I do some mental mathematics. Each person is spending about a minute with Amma. Five hundred divided by sixty. It will be eight hours before it is my turn to go up and have Amma bless me.

I decide to leave. As I pull into my driveway I am a little disappointed with myself for not staying and receiving the formal blessing. I get out of the car. A little light headed, but aware of the present moment. As I turn toward my front door I see a red fox sitting at the doorstep. Not near the door, but at the door. He is looking directly at me. Thin, black feet, and beautiful auburn red coat of fur. His long, thick tail stretches out like a flag. Alert, attentive, but not scared. He sits as I approach. When I am within three feet I suddenly have the strangest idea. I want to talk to him. Since I don't speak "fox" I decide to simply use English. I ask sincerely, "Can I help you in some way?" He instantly gets up and moves around the front of the house. Intrigued, I follow.

The fox moves directly, without hesitation, to a metal bird bath that I have sitting on the ground. I can already see that the bird bath is empty. I grab a hose, turn on the water and walk slowly towards the fox and bird bath. I don't want to scare him. But this is not an issue. He sits there waiting for me to come over and fill the bird bath. Then, he drinks.

This is not a domestic fox. I have never fed it nor seen it before. And while I have had many encounters with wild animals I have never spoken to one before and received an immediate answer. Then it occurs to me. Even though Amma never touched me physically I was in her presence. Amma represents Divine Mother. On her web site she explains: "The mightiest force in the cosmos is the silent power of Divine Mother's pure love."

It seems no coincidence that I should not only encounter, but have communion with a red fox. Because of my encounter with Amma my energy signature temporarily changed to enable this interaction. The fox is the totem symbol of feminine magic and kundalini energy. The hair and fur of the fox are symbols of feminine energy and fertility. Great masters of camouflage, fox can effortlessly blend in with their surroundings. It is the camouflage of the foxes that is one of the first journeys we must recognize and move through in order to see nature in it's truest light.

Foxes teach us how to control our aura, our energy field in such a way that we can blend in and harmonize with others. Usually seen at dawn and dusk, the fox is viewed as having supernatural powers. These times are known as "between time". When the magical world of animals, and the world that we live in, intersect. Some of the greatest learning for humankind comes from not only connecting with, but understanding the tremendous gifts of nature.

Humans and Nature

For thousands of years people have seen the universe, our planet, and nature, as being distinctively separate from the human experience. With this separation in place the human species decided long ago that we can, and should, consume every available resource – animals, plants, minerals - to create and manifest our vision of reality.

Thomas Jefferson penned the opening of the U.S. Declaration of Independence. "We hold these truths to be self-evident, that all men are created equal; that they are endowed by their Creator with inherent and inalienable rights that among these, are life, liberty, and the pursuit of happiness … " This sentence remains one of the most profound statements verifying the equality and rights of all humans.

It echoes the Buddhist writings and ceremonies that pronounce: "May all beings be happy." Many branches of Buddhism, for example Tibetan and Japanese, have a broader interpretation of what encompasses a sentient being. They include animals, plants and inanimate objects. The Declaration of Independence, of course, does not have a direct proclamation for the rights of nature. On a global scale we see that the separation between humans and nature creates significant imbalance in global ecosystems.

The collective consciousness is slowly getting and spreading a message that flags the issue. Global warming has shifted from a vague scientific hypothesis to a widely accepted fact among scientists and the general public. Disney, the champion of feel good films, sends out messages that are about environmental stewardship. As early as 1937 with Snow White and The Seven Dwarfs, by escaping into the forest with its friendly animals and dwarfs, Snow White symbolically shows us that harmony exists in nature.

The theme of the precarious balance between nature and humankind continues with a string of hits including Bambi (1942), The Jungle Book (1967), The Lion King (1994), Pocahontas (1995), Tarzan (1999), Finding Nemo (2003) and WALL·E. By the time WALL·E hits theaters the symbolism has been replaced by direct storyline. If you were wondering, WALL·E stands for Waste, Allocation, Load Lifter - Earth class. The message is simple. Earth becomes a barren wasteland as humankind continues it obsession with using natural resources to create an endless supply of materialistic objects which ultimately become garbage (waste) and extinguish all life on the planet with the exception of one small seedling that provides a minuscule, yet hopeful sign of redemption for all species.

Almost at the exact same time that WALL·E was in theaters getting children to ponder this potential timeline; adults were opening the doors on the Svalbard Global Seed Vault. Alternately referred to as The New Noah's Arc, or the Doomsday Vault, the very high-tech project maintains around 10 million seeds from every country in the world in a vault located deep in a mountain in the north of mainland Norway. A 125m tunnel drops into the earth. It ends at three vaults. Air locked doors with keypad entry and stone and plastic-impregnated concrete walls. While the temperature of the air has been cooled to between -18C and -20C, Norwegian meteorologists have calculated that even without power, these vaults will still be below freezing 200 years from now. With these cold conditions peas could last for 2,000 years . Sorghum 20,000 years. This science fiction meets reality project is designed to preserve crops in the face of climate change, war and natural disasters.

The Ancients Are Still Alive

On a cold, sunny December afternoon I walk through Sequoia National Park. Giant sequoias grow naturally only on the west slope of the Sierra Nevada in California. The scientific name is *Sequoiadendron giganteum*. Because of it's enormous volume of wood, the Giant Sequoia stands alone as the largest living creature on planet Earth. Of the world's 37 largest sequoia trees, 20 are giant sequoias growing in Sequoia and Kings Canyon.

The snow packed trail is surrounded by these enormous and ancient creatures. It is hard to know where to focus my eyes and my attention. All around me soaring sequoia trees stand like monuments. Beautiful auburn red trunks push dramatically out of the snow covered ground. Young trees stand with green branches that lusciously complement the color of their larger companions, possibly their parents. Each time I stop my eyes naturally float skyward. Small patches of blue sky fight like puzzle pieces to be noticed amongst the vast canopy of these huge trees. It takes about thirty minutes to reach the tree I am looking for.

His name is General Sherman. Born before Christ, he is 2,700 years old. Possibly the largest living creature on Earth. He is a living skyscraper. As I approach everything else in sight disappears. There is a short, split rail fence separating the trail from General Sherman. The park is empty today. I climb over the fence and approach General Sherman. Not only is his physical presence mind boggling; he also has a strong energetic presence.

I kneel down in the snow and lay a hand on his skin. It is smooth. Perhaps because so many other people have touched this tree. General Sherman's largest branch is almost seven feet in diameter. A single arm wider than a person is tall. And each year General Sherman adds enough wood to his already massive frame to create a 60-foot-tall tree of usual proportions.

Silently I thank this creature for his presence and endurance. For providing and guarding offspring. A tree this old has had many children. Even more, he has lived through millennium. Civilizations have risen and fallen many times while this silent giant has quietly and simply lived his life. How many sun rises, blizzards, storms and even visitations by humans has General Sherman witnessed? "Most of the Sierra trees die of disease, fungi," John Muir wrote. "But nothing hurts the Big Trees. Barring accidents, it seems to be immortal."

Eagle – A Shaman Teaches About Nature

About a year before my encounter with General Sherman I actively study nature's mysteries and gifts with a Lakota shaman. I sit in his small, but beautifully decorated teaching room, looking out the window. As usual, the conversation moves quickly and in different directions. Like all great teachers, his words were merely a vehicle for deeper understanding of timeless truths. We talk about the ideal role and relationship between humans and nature. I say, "Perhaps one reason man has been so arrogant is because we are at the top of the food chain."

Eagle looks at me with a glance which suggests, "Is what you said really the truth?" As a teacher this provides an opening. It doesn't say, "You are wrong." That would close down the energy. After this look he says, "Why do you think we're at the top of the food chain?"

I know I am in trouble. My mind simultaneously races through all the reasons I said what I did and all the reasons it might be wrong. All I can think of is the common understanding. "Well, for one, we eat everything else."

Eagle points out the window. "What about that tree right there?" I look and see that he's pointing at a rather modest pine tree.

"Yes," I say, just waiting for the rest.

"Well, it is probably two hundred years old." He smiles. "It will probably live at least another hundred. That's three times longer than you will probably live. Perhaps this tree is at the top of the food chain."

I carried the intellectual understanding of what Eagle said for over a year before I touched General Sherman. Then I was able to have both an emotional and energetic understanding of what he taught.

The Four Worlds

Eagle's teachings cover a lot of territory. Dreaming, names and numbers, masks, healing, choreography of energy, circles of movement. Some of his teachings are formalized for groups and required practice and study. Other teachings are spontaneous and for one individual. One of the most significant teachings for me is an appreciation and understanding of the four worlds. Many Native American and shamanic traditions relay an understanding of different worlds that co-exist on our planet. I will relay my understanding of the four worlds as simply as I can. In no specific order of importance the four worlds are animal, plant, mineral and human.

The Animal World

North is the direction of the animal world. No one really knows how many animal species exist. In 1995, the United Nations' published the Global Biodiversity Assessment. An ambitious undertaking, the document indicates there are 13.6 million species on Earth. Some field scientists dismiss this number. They believe that there may be as many as 30 million species of tropical insects and as many as 100 million species of animals. While this debate may continue for decades, it is indisputable that *we are losing species.*

The current sickness of our planet is seen most dramatically with the extinction of entire species of animals. Humans caused the extinction of the turkey sized dodo bird back in 1861. We have lost at least 500 species of animals because of human activity. Today there are about 5,000 endangered animals and at least one species dies out every year. One reason for this decline is that our relationship with the animal world has changed.

Human consciousness has shifted animals from their role as partners in the process of natural order and harmony into commodities. What do I mean by commodity? Quite simply animals have become objects for human use. How else could we have investment vehicles that include options trading on pork belly futures? A report from the United Kingdom shows that in the U.K. 97% of animals are slaughtered and consumed as food. That is approximately 12 animals for every person in the UK each year. Possibly worse is the fact that thirty five percent of the world's grain is grown specifically to feed livestock instead of people. Animals and plants are no longer viewed by humans as kin, but rather as products.

The Plant World

South is the direction of the plant world. There are about 375,000 species of plants, with more being discovered each year. This includes seed plants, bryophytes, ferns and relatives of ferns called fern allies. Plants consist of two main groups; green algae and land plants. For millennium humans have recognized that of all the valuable services provided by plants, the healing properties are significant.

The Mineral World

West is the direction of the mineral world. Minerals are holders and transformers. There are currently more than 4,000 known minerals, according to the International Mineralogical Association, which is responsible for the approval of and naming of new mineral species found in nature. In a podcast on the USGS (United States Geological Survey) web site, Kathleen Johnson, USGS Mineral Resources Program Coordinator, agrees, "Mineral materials are the building blocks of everything we use. Everyone living on earth depends on mineral materials to create products that support our way of life, our health, and the global economy."

The Human World

East is the direction of the human world. Humans are stewards of the other worlds.

The Four Worlds Are Everywhere

If we step back and look at Planet Earth from a macro viewpoint we can see clearly that there is the land below our feet containing all of the various minerals. Animals encompass every species with the exception of humans. Plants are, well, plants. And then there's us. The first thing to consider is that each of these worlds has special properties that make them unique. In fact their uniqueness is so complete that we easily distinguish the four groups. The other thing we might notice is that all four worlds have representation everywhere on the planet. You can be in Japan or Peru or Bali or Germany and you will find minerals, plants, animals and humans.

This simple truth sometimes astonishes me. I am at a conference in Toronto. My hotel is a big hotel in the middle of the city. During a break I am lounging on a recliner at the pool courtyard which was on the eighth floor. Two ravens fly and land in one of the potted trees in the courtyard. Instantly I see all four worlds. The birds, the trees, and the minerals which are now realized as the concrete form of this building, and the people at the pool. The four worlds are everywhere.

From an ecological point-of-view each world carries equal significance. Humans have no more importance than minerals. This is a perspective that we have not yet fully embraced; but one which is required if we are going to be stewards of the planet.

The relationship between these four worlds goes beyond acknowledging their existence. Each of these worlds is literally intertwined with the others. Consider, for example, your own body. If you ate dinner last night you probably consumed all four worlds. The plants known as vegetables grow from the nutrients in the ground. Other plants are processed into pasta, bread, tea and coffee. Meat and fish come from animals that also eat vegetables. That's three worlds right there.

Did you consume a human? Probably. There's a high probability that some aspect of the human world — from urine and solid waste to even decomposed bodies — has filtered it's way into the chain that became your dinner. On top of that you probably were breathing while you ate thanks to the life giving oxygen that plants provide and you might have gone so far as to swallow a vitamin pill filled with mineral supplements.

This is an example of the interdependent relationship in terms of food and constitution. The four worlds hold court in all arenas. Consider your home. Our living quarters are home to all four worlds. Minerals loaded in everything from copper and aluminum plumbing and wiring to drywall and ceramic tiles. Plants maintain a presence in wood frames and furniture culled from trees to the plants that we lovingly water both inside and outside our property. Animals are present not only in natural fibers but pets, and the numerous little creatures like spiders and dust mites who have taken up residence as nonpaying guests. We are the human element. The first recognition of the ever present nature of the four worlds is almost an intellectual exercise — constantly seeing and perceiving the worlds. On the heels of this awareness is an emotional and energetic understanding of the critical, inseparable relationship.

We Are All One

The wind is outrageous. I see gusts of wind embodied by snow moving across the mountains. I feel the wind is alive. A force with life in and of itself, like a form of energy that carries it's own life. I shared my experience in my next session with Eagle.

"Yes," he says. "In Native American languages different elements, like the wind, do have spirit. It is called "Manitou" by some tribes. But the essence of all spirit still contains all the four worlds. Fire, for example, when it burns it uses air. And from the wood itself there are minerals and plants embedded. Everything contains everything in it." The interdependency between the worlds is comprehensive. We are all one and the same. The other worlds become us and we become them. Not only are the four worlds everywhere in their own form; they are everywhere in every form!

Further, each of the four worlds has four distinct subdivisions. At the same time that everything is the same, especially at the atomic level, there are layers and layers of individualization. The universe continues to expand. It will contract, but right now it is expanding. In this expansion it takes on endless expressions of being. Here is the first division:

THE ANIMAL WORLD	THE MINERAL WORLD
Four legged animals	Gems
Birds	Crystals
Swimming animals	Sands
Crawlers	Rocks
THE PLANT WORLD	**THE HUMAN WORLD**
Fruits and vegetables	Yellow
Trees	White
Grasses	Red
Bushes	Black

As Above, So Below

Many spiritual paths use this simple phrase – *as above, so below* – to describe the mirrored relationship between the macrocosm and the microcosm. Between the universe, solar system and what happens on Earth. I believe every person on the planet recognizes that the huge forces of nature created us. There is no contradiction adding God into the mixture because if God isn't a huge force of nature then we have a problem. Creation is so perfect that most of us only get glimpses of the perfection, the harmony, the infallibility of the puzzle. Nature is one of the lenses that we can use to decipher and admire the complex precision of which we play a role. One model for simultaneously viewing the macro and microcosm uses the compass.

NORTH

The Stars are the Guardian. They provide seeds. A spark of consciousness through time

EAST

The Sun is the Scout. The sun illuminates and scouts time. It allows us to see time.

SOUTH

The Moon is the Provider. It gives us our time (the 28 day cycle). It provides time and the water we exist in. The moon creates the waves

WEST

The Earth is the Keeper. The Earth stores time. It records time in it's body just like trees have rings that record their personal history. Our physical bodies are also time keepers.

Now consider seasons. Every place on the planet has seasons. In the northern and southern hemispheres seasons are visually more apparent as temperatures shift. But even at the equator there are seasons. Usually the variation appears more in terms of rainfall. The seasons are created by the forces of nature as the tilting of the Earth's axis toward and away from the sun changes the dynamics of the natural world. Winter, spring, summer, fall.

Remember how many aspects of nature appear in fours. The four seasons provide a coloring of time. We see visual changes. This coloring of time is Mother Nature's way of steering all of Earth's species toward linking to the sacred spiral. The sacred spiral is an ancient symbol of growth, transformation and evolution. It represents divine energy and the ongoing cycle of life including death and rebirth. We have a direct link and relationship to the spirals of the planets and the stars.

The four seasons have spiritual purposes which are reflected in what happens in nature. Nature's division of the year into quarters provides an external reflection to what we experience as our own internal lessons. In fact, nature always provides these lessons. Remember a time when you experienced nature demonstrating intensity. A blizzard, thunderstorm, hail storm, searing heat or freezing cold. While nature is doing it's thing how do you feel? Are you calm. Nervous. Irritated. Joyful. Your internal reaction to the external manifestation of nature is one of the quickest ways to gauge not only what is going on in your life and your reaction to it; but also to recognize and work on the related lesson.

Seasons provide a more measured version of the same process. In winter certain animals hibernate. Winter is a time for introspection. We can use this quiet time when the days are short to seed our ideas. Spring is a time of birth and renewal. Animals give birth and plants sprout. It is a time when we bring forth growth that has been germinating. Summer is full of life. It is a time of movement. Young animals begin to step out on their own. People are active and spend time outdoors. Fall moves us again toward temporary death as leaves begin falling off trees. Farmers, know and rely on the natural movement of the seasons.

In 1792 Robert B. Thomas publishes *The Farmers Almanac*. Thomas believed that the weather on Earth was influenced by sunspots — magnetic storms on the surface of the sun. The methodology has been refined over the years. The publishers state: "We believe that nothing in the universe happens haphazardly; that there is a cause and effect pattern to all phenomena." The Almanac continues to offer weather forecasts, tide times and heights, relationships of the planets, phases of the moon, temperature and precipitation deviations. For many farmers this publication is as important as a Bible. The phases of farming are similar to the phases of the seasons. Seeding, planting, harvesting, preparation for winter.

The planets, sun, moon and earth all play a role in this dance. In fact, every day provides us a miniature version of what happens over the course of the full year. The sun rises giving birth to a new day. We live in the day. We use the evening to get quiet; and we hibernate during the nighttime. Nature too moves in accordance to the energy of the day. Wildlife photographers, fishermen and hunters all know that very early in the morning and just at dusk or twilight are the times of greatest movement for animals. What is less known is that human egos drop down between three and six p.m. and twelve and two a.m. If you happen to be out in nature at this time you have an opportunity to access and communicate with nature more easily than at other times.

The tides are created by a gravitational tug-of-war between the sun, moon, and the Earth. All objects in the universe exert a gravitational impact on each other. As above, so below. The closer they are to each other, or the larger they are physically, the stronger this pull. Each of the planets creates gravitational pull on the Earth. But the draw of the moon and sun are more noticeable because the moon is physically so close, and the sun is so large. How large you ask? The Earth is about the size of the average sun spot. If the sun was a container we could drop 1,300,000 Earths into it. The sun contains 99.8% of the mass of the entire solar system. That is big.

To the Chinese, the sun and the moon have been considered "chief objects of veneration," according to writings that date back to emperor Wu Di (157-87 B.C.) of the Han dynasty. The highest tides, which are known as spring tides, occur when these three bodies - the earth, moon and sun - are aligned in a straight line.

The moon also gives us lunar phases. Dark moon, new moon; waxing crescent moon, first quarter moon, waxing gibbous moon, full moon, waning gibbous moon, last quarter moon, waning crescent moon. The time between two full moons is 29.53 days (29 days, 12 hours, 44 minutes). Each aspect of the moons phase has a corresponding phase and impact on natural cycles on Earth (and on us). Farmers use phases of the moon for farming. They plant seeds within a few days of a full moon for faster germination. And they rarely plant on the day of the new moon or full moon. In addition to controlling the tides, it is believed that the moon also influences water tables within the soil and sap within plants. Combined with moonlight itself, this impacts growth rates of plants.

The Energetic Impact of the Full Moon

Farmers and plants aren't the only ones who are impacted by the phases of the moon. Werewolves go berserk during a full moon. In my personal experience people do become agitated during the full moon. Communication suffers. The word lunatic describes someone who is mentally off balance. Energetically, the emotions of humans are received and transmitted back from the moon, like a giant mirror, down onto the surface of the ocean and the planet. The full moon provides a unique opportunity for spiritual development. There is a large amount of energy pouring down.

Some full moons carry more energy than others. The Wesak full moon is the first full moon in the month of May. This is the full moon of Scorpio. Wesak is a celebration of Buddha's birth, enlightenment and death. It is perhaps the most important day in the Buddhist calendar. While Wesak is celebrated around the world, there is also a formal celebration in the Wesak Valley in the Himalayas.

There is also a Christian slant to Wesak. For some it is known as a time during which Christ gathers the spiritual hierarchy together in meditation. The Buddha, representing these forces, appears and blesses humanity. The combining of these two spiritual traditions is no accident. Indeed, as participants around the globe mediate on this full moon the energy is quite profound.

Animals Are Messengers

I bend down to step inside. The adobe framed door is only about five feet in height. Almost instantly the brilliant sunlight disappears and is replaced by the warm glow of semi white walls that are lit from a kiva fireplace. It is quite a contrast to the exterior where this shop and living quarters are one of many rooms attached to the larger complex of the Taos pueblo.

While construction of some aspects of the all adobe buildings began in the 1400's, the architecture itself looks incredibly modern. Walls, sometimes three feet thick, keep not only the light, but the heat of the sun at bay in summertime. This is incredibly useful as the people who live at the pueblo do not use electricity or running water. The people here are of the Tewa tribe. Translated, *Tewa* means red willow. And this is quite obvious as there are numerous red willow trees perched alongside the pristine creek that runs directly through the pueblo.

I immediately scan the room. It is neither large, nor crowded. In fact the only thing I see are a few pieces of art on the wall. But this art is different than anything else I have seen. They are pieces made with wood and leather and bird feathers. Small, like the size of a book. Even in the dim light I can see how colorful the feathers are. As I walk towards a small piece the artist walks in from a back room. He wears a large face filled with a polite smile.

"My name is Daniel, and this is my work," he says.

"It's beautiful."

Suddenly the smile seems more genuine. "Thank you. They are feathers from around the world. Because I am native I can buy these feathers. Each bird has it's own significance."

The piece I am looking at has several black-blue feathers that are cut like jewels coming out of a small piece of wood with a bird symbol. Then, below the wood, one small feather hangs down from a piece of leather. This feather is stunning and combines brilliant blue with green. I've never seen one like it. "I like this one," I pronounce, even though I haven't looked at the others.

"That one has a special story," Daniel shares. "My father passed about a year ago. I was sad about it for a long time. He taught me so many things. About two month ago I was sitting under a tree. Sleeping. I had a dream about my father," Daniel pauses for a moment as if he is reliving the dream to remember it.

"He came to me and he told me he was fine. He was happy. That I should not be upset. That I need to continue on my own journey. Then he walked away into a cloud. When I woke I noticed a magpie sitting in the tree in front of me. This bird had left three feathers on the ground right beside me. I knew this was a message that the dream was real. Those are the feathers. The feather on the bottom I bought. It is a macaw feather."

I bought the piece immediately. Not only was it a beautiful story but I had recently learned that one of my own totem animals is the magpie. It was a perfect gift to myself. Now it sits above my bed to help me with clarity of my dreams.

About a month later I have a session with Eagle. I bring in the feathered artwork and tell him the story. He thinks for a minute and says, "There is something in your aura about the sound of the word macaw. You should say this word over the next week and see if it brings anything." I want to ask him more about this mysterious meaning but he grabs his coat. Apparently we are going somewhere. Eagle looks at me, "You drive."

We are not driving anywhere in particular. There is no destination. I am simply driving. A mini road trip. A medicine journey. I turn down some mountain roads. Roads that weave like the streams. After twenty minutes I come to a fork in the road. Straight ahead is a little field that sits before the Cache la Poudre river. I drive into the field and stop because I see five horses. They are quite stunning in this setting. Very wild west.

We just sit and look at the horses. Finally Eagle turns to me. "You see the white one?"

"Yes." There is only one white horse so it's hard not to notice.

"She just told me she's pregnant."

"What?" I knew that Eagle could talk with animals but I am surprised since the communication is happening right in front of me and I don't hear anything. Just as I am thinking about the many ramifications of his statement the horse starts walking over to the car. The Hyundai SUV is pretty tall. Enough that the passenger side window is at horse height. The horse sticks his head right in the window. Eagle starts petting it. I can't believe my eyes and simply look at the big horse head. Suddenly it jerks it's head back out the window.

"Oh, don't worry," Eagle says. My heart slows down until I realize that he is not talking to me. "He is O.K.," Eagle continues. "Come back." The horse moves back to the car and sticks his head in one more time.

Watch For The Interaction

These events became part of my personal experience and learning about the animal world. Learning that the way we normally see, interpret and communicate with this amazing world is extremely limited. The limitation, which is our own viewpoint, prevents us from accepting the amazing gifts which are freely offered. Learning to speak with and listen to animals does not require special DNA, or multiple viewings of *Doctor Doolittle*.

Chief Dan George was both a talented actor and chief of the Tsleil-waututh Nation of Burrard Inlet, British Columbia. You may know Chief George because he received an Academy Award nomination for his supporting role as an Indian who adopts Dustin Hoffman in Arthur Penn's *Little Big Man* (1970). He was comfortable in different worlds. This famous quote describes his appreciation and knowledge of the animal world.

> *"If you talk to the animals they will talk with you and you will know each other. If you do not talk to them you will not know them, and what you do not know you will fear. What one fears one destroys."*

To communicate with the animal world you need to start with the perspective that animals are not subordinate to humans. And, begin to cultivate an awareness of their unique capabilities and the messages they carry to us. Indeed, just as the seasons and the weather are external messengers, so are animals. The trick is to pay attention.

Daniel's magpie visited him in the real world as a confirmation of the message from his father in a dream. The horses that visited Eagle and myself in our mutual day dream carried a message of communication. Horse legends tell that horses have powers of clairvoyance and can recognize individuals who are involved in magic. Horses, because of their movement, are strong messengers of travel and journeying.

Any animal can come to you in many different ways. You can see animals in your dreams. In nature, the zoo, books, television, the Internet. It does not have to be a "real world" experience to count as an encounter. What is important is that you recognize when you see an animal. Too

often animals are in our presence but we don't see th
thing to do. Start looking.

Animal Totems and the Messages They Carry

How do you know what the message is? Every animal has uniq
teristics. These may be natural strengths, senses, abilities for hunt.
or escaping as prey.   While it is certainly not the best environmei
most animals, you can clearly see some of these traits when you visit a z
Elephants, leopards, prairie dogs, seals, bats. You can see and sense hov,
they have innate instincts, movements and abilities.

Sometimes the traits are quite obvious. Cats, for example, are widely
recognized as being independent, clever, unpredictable and playful – even in
hunting. If you have a cat, or encounter them, you will know whether the
cat is teaching or sharing with you it's skills and abilities. Notice whether you
can use the abilities of independence and playfulness to your advantage. Here
is a simplified version of a few common animals and their characteristics:

Animal	Characteristic
Bear	Introspection and strength
Buffalo	Abundance and prayer
Butterfly	Transformation and grace
Coyote	Humor and adaptability
Dog	Courage, friendship and love
Dolphin	Wisdom and harmony
Eagle	Spiritual enlightenment and transcendence
Elk	Stamina and friendship
Fox	Cleverness and invisibility
Horse	Inner power and freedom
Hummingbird	Boundless joy and agility
Owl	Insight and psychic vision
Rabbit	Fertility and new life
Snake	Rebirth and wisdom
Squirrel	Trust and playfulness

The traits of certain animals have been enhanced through mythology
and culture. Consider the spider. Their mythology ranges around the
world and through the ages. In fact entire books are written about the

ery, ability and magic of spiders. The Vedic scriptures of ancient India npare Creation to a spider's web. The spider creates the web and then es in its creation.

Similarly, God is both the container of the universe and everything that is contained in it. In South Africa, tales describe how gods used spider webs to travel to and from heaven. Native American cultures have various interpretations of the spider. One is as grandmother who not only weaves creation, but links the past and the future.

Sometimes your encounter with an animal is practically an intervention. In other words the animal comes directly up to you. You can't avoid noticing it because the encounter is out of the normal pattern that you would expect. The animal energetically picks up a signal that enables it to visit with you. How does this work? Unlike humans, animals don't control or block the flow of prana with intentions or stories from their mind. Because energy is flowing without restriction they more rapidly pick up signals from their environment, including a signal to come visit. This is an attraction on the spiritual level and the reason that animals are spirit guides that can convey specific wisdom.

When this type of intervention with an animal occurs in nature you should **note what was on your mind just before the encounter.** The thought that you were having relates to the message this animal is bringing you. Take the characteristics of the animal and relate them to your mental story to see what lesson you can learn.

The animal world is ever present. As a result we have ongoing opportunities to examine our encounters and the wisdom that is offered. When you make a connection with an animal (in person or not) use your intuitive understanding of the characteristics and wisdom of that animal to see if there is a lesson or advice. Just as we receive teachings from attractions and repulsions to other people, an affinity or a fear of an animal also suggests that a lesson is available.

Plants are Healers

If animals are spirit guides, barometers of our internal state; then plants are paramedics. The nature of the plant world is to grow and to heal.

Consider chocolate. The Mayan civilization worshiped the cacao tree. It was sacred. They named it cacahuaquchtl, believing the pods were a gift to man from the Gods. Ancient drawings show cacao pods being used

during rituals and ceremonies; and writings describ~
prepare cocoa creating drinks ranging from a thin liqu
We now know that Chocolate derived from cacao conta
It also boosts serotonin which is the chemical in our brain ı
mood. You probably know of the healing nature of several otı.

- ➢ **Garlic** can improve blood lipids and may reduce the risk of blc
- ➢ **Red Tea** for it's antioxidant properties
- ➢ **St John's Wort** for mild depression
- ➢ **Cranberry juice** helps fight urinary tract infections
- ➢ **Valerian** is a mild sedative and can help with insomnia
- ➢ **Eucalyptus oil** provides relief for congestion and coughs

This is a small fraction of your daily encounter with plants that have been used to formulate products and medicines. Take a close look at the ingredients in your shampoo, body products, cleaning supplies. Tea tree leaf oil, lavender, sunflower seed oil, coconut.

Since the dawn of mankind plants have been known to have properties that heal. Herbology is the science, the art, of using plants for healing. Herbalists use medicinal plants to create changes in the physical body that allows the body to heal itself. The plants and their mixtures can be swallowed, ingested, or applied externally. Many civilizations designate the knowledge and the talents for using plant medicine to specific individuals. Medicine men. It doesn't matter if they are from China, Africa, Australia or any other part of the world. Their skills are based upon using the natural healing properties of plants to stabilize a variety of conditions.

Mother nature has such incredible healing intelligence that almost every injury or disease that is specific to a geographic environment already provides the healing plants for those conditions. Consider the Aloe Vera plant. It is commonly found in the warm, dry climates of Africa, and the western United States. Known around the world for it's ability to soothe and heal burns and sunburns, the plant grows in exactly the location it is needed most. Everything you need to heal yourself may already grow in your own backyard.

Plants at Your Disposal

As one of the four worlds, plants are ever present in our life. Look around your living room. Take a walk outside. Visit a flower store. As with

ials, the secret of plants is learning how to access their innate proper-
... This is part study, part intuition. The study is to learn the proper-
es of specific plants. There are many common plants and trees that have
properties that are readily available without studying chemistry.

The most common drug in the world is aspirin. Guess where it comes
from? The willow tree. Romans first recorded the use of willow bark as
a fever fighter. The leaves and bark of the tree contain a substance called
salicin. This is a naturally occurring compound that is similar to acetylsalicylic acid which is the chemical name for aspirin. Not until the 1800's
did scientists discover that salicylic acid is the substance in the tree that re-
lieves fever and pain. Then in 1897 German chemist Felix Hoffmann was
looking for something to relieve his father's arthritis. He studied French
chemist Charles Gergardt's experiments and "rediscovered" acetylsalicylic
acid. This is the aspirin we use today. Nature meets science.

What is not as common knowledge is that if you have a headache and
simply sit underneath a willow tree the medicinal properties of the tree
can alleviate your headache. Popping a pill is more convenient; but ques-
tionably faster. The healing properties of plants are energetic. Proximity
to a plant is one way to infuse your body with healing properties.

Costa Rica, - Feeling Plant Energy in a Cloud Forest

Like people, plants have energetic signatures. Auras. People that are
sensitive to energy can feel plant energy. Some people can see it. The
energy fields of plants expand after it rains. My wife and I are travelling in
Costa Rica. Translated as "rich coast", the country is filled with rainforests.
The interior is as rich as the coastline. According to one legend, when the
Spanish were exploring the coast in the early 1500's they believed they saw
gold hanging from the trees. Rich Coast was not an inappropriate name.

Some of the forests in Costa Rica receive more than 200 inches of rain
per year. Jungles that drink water. The spectacular Monteverde Cloud
Forest is one such place. It is a cloud forest because its elevation enshrines
the forest in clouds on a regular basis. We arrive as dusk settles in. In this
country arriving anywhere at night in the countryside involves some risk.
The risk is that you will either get lost, or the road conditions, especially
during the rainy season, are so bad that a pothole can swallow your car.
I see in the fading light one thing. Trees. Such a large number of trees

that the little lodge we are staying at looks like a child'
miniscule compared to the environment. We are stayi..
house in the town of approximately two hundred souls. \
quickly is that this guest house, like most of the town, is .
"friends." Friends, in this case, are Quakers.

Quaker faith holds there is an inner light in every person th
of Gods divine nature. Friends believe in direct, unmediated comm
with the Divine. They also believe in a commitment to living a life
outwardly reflects this inward experience. William Penn is one famo.
representative of the Quakers. In his book *Some Fruits of Solitude,* published
in 1693, he states the importance of nature: "It were Happy if we studied Nature more in natural Things; and acted according to Nature; whose
rules are few, plain and most reasonable. Let us begin where she begins,
go her Pace, and close always where she ends, and we cannot miss of being
good Naturalists."

In 1951 a group of Quakers decided that conscientious objection to
the Korean War would prevent them from accepting the draft. Most
Quakers consider themselves pacifists. They emigrated to Costa Rica and
settled Monteverde. The Quakers started a cheese factory and a Friends
School. With ecological foresight they purchased much of the land that
constitutes the Monteverde Reserve.

My wife and I decide to take our adventure and experience directly
into the forest. There are a few designated walking trails. We want something richer and decide to backpack into the rain forest for a couple of
days. We learn there is a remote cabin you can hike to. The Quakers agree
to help us and prepare food for our journey.

We leave early in the morning as the jungle begins to wake up. This
is heaven. Everywhere you turn there is a different view and experience.
Look up and there is a canopy of green like a natural cathedral. Bend
down and there is a trail of leaf cutter ants moving their caravan across the
trail. Many of the small, crawling creatures are more deadly than anything
the size of a human. Stand up and see orchids, bromeliads, ferns, vines,
and mosses lining up on top of tall trees like decorations. The air is full of
noises, the flurry of leaves falling and animals moving.

The cabin is a one-room, wooden building that sits in the middle of
a little clearing. The roof seems to be falling in and the porch looks un-
stable. It looks like it might be more dangerous to sleep inside the cabin
than outside. Nevertheless it is getting dark and beginning to rain. Inside

oden framed bed racks await. We unroll our sleeping bags and try to make sure we don't disturb any sleeping bugs or rodents. I have not seen a rodent yet; but I know they are going to be large like everything else in this country. Unwrapping the first brown paper bag provided by the Quakers we discover that dinner is a cheese sandwich and a bottle of apple juice.

About three in the morning I wake up and have to go to the bathroom. This consumes my mind for fifteen minutes. Can I possibly wait until morning comes? I can't. I am fully dressed so all I have to do is find my boots. I shake them out just to make sure a scorpion hasn't settled in. I grab my flashlight and head outside. It is still drizzling but partial moon-light puts a mysterious glow on the clearing. Looking cautiously around I move toward a tree. I turn around and see tiny, shiny eyeballs glowing at me. Three white opossum sized creatures slide into the forest. It is time to get back into my sleeping bag. I stop. Beside me is an enormous plant. It is at least thirty feet tall; but it is not a tree. It is a fern. A Jurassic Park fern. More than just it's size I am attracted to the energy it has. I can feel this fern from three feet away. It is like a presence that is extending it's essence outward. This is my first experience with the aura of a plant.

Two days and eight cheese sandwiches later we reluctantly hike back to the village. Surprisingly, the Quakers ask us if we would join their next group meeting and consider staying in Monteverde to teach English to the children. It is an offer that is filled with honor. In a short period of time I feel like we have become, to a limited degree, Friends.

Essential Oils Are the Essence of Plants

There are different ways the healing properties of plants can impact your physical body. Right up there with touching, eating and drinking is the use of essential oils as a tonic that can lubricate and heal your body. Essential oils are liquids distilled from various parts of a plant - leaves, stems, flow-ers, bark, even roots. They are literally the *essence* of the plant. There are hundreds of different essential oils available for purchase. I would like to share with you a few of the essential oils that I use. Pure essential oils are so strong that you only need a few drops to create a noticeable impact. You should not take them internally; and if you are pregnant or have skin allergies you should consult a physician.

Black Pepper

Even pepper can be distilled into oil. Black Pepper oil can
grounded by rubbing a few drops on the souls of your feet. Ma
practices involve moving energy through the higher chakras. Blac.
is a nice compliment. I like to use it after meditation, a Reiki session
a bath with lavender oil, as a way to create balance.

Eucalyptus

As an ointment eucalyptus can be used for the immune, respiratory, and
skin system. The oil has properties that are cooling, stimulating and pen-
etrating. As such it is frequently used to help with respiratory issues; and
you can put a few drops into water that you boil on the stove to open up
the air in the room. Often it is used in health club steam rooms to add a
healing property as well as a nice smell to the vapor. Eucalyptus supports
emotional balance. With it's history it has become a household remedy in
Australia. The leaves and the oil have been used for respiratory ailments
including bronchitis and croup. Even fever related conditions (malaria,
typhoid, cholera) and skin problems like burns, ulcers and wounds.

Frankincense and Myrrh

In the Middle East frankincense is considered a holy oil. It has been part
of religious ceremonies for thousands of years. What were the gifts the
wise men gave in honor of the birth of Jesus? Matheww 2:11 states: *"And
when they were come into the house, they saw the young child with Mary, his mother,
and fell down, and worshipped him: and when they had opened their treasures, they
presented unto him gifts: **gold**, and **frankincense**, and **myrrh**."* These three
distinct and timeless treasures inspire merchants to move along ancient
trade routes for millennia.

Frankincense was used during the time of Christ for anointing and
healing. Today European hospitals use frankincense therapeutically.
Frankincense is strong in sesquiterpenes, which are found naturally in
plants and insects as defensive agents or pheromones. Frankincense is
stimulating, and it helps overcome stress and supports the immune system.

e sesquiterpenes also help erase DNA damage and supply oxygen to tis-
es which can be excellent for cancer patients. It is strong and dilution
is recommended even for topical usage.

Myrrh refers to the resinous dried sap of a number of trees. The most common source of myrrh grows natively in Somalia and also in eastern Ethiopia. Myrrh was enormously valuable in the time of the Roman Empire when Jesus was born. It was burned during funerals until the 15th century. Today, myrrh is used in oral hygiene products, mouthwashes, cosmetics and soaps. As an essential oil can help with meditation, and with arthritis, asthma, bronchitis, gum infections, coughs and sore throats.

Lavender

Lavender is a must have. Lavender has calming properties. At night before bed you can put a little lavender oil on your solar plexus to help calm down any issues you may be dealing with. Put a dozen drops of lavender oil into your bath water. Lavender can cleanse common cuts and abrasions. Part of the modern story of essential oils comes from the intersection of science, nature and accident.

While working in the laboratory of his family's perfumery business, French scientist Rene Gattefosse, severely burned his hand and forearm. As the story goes just at that moment one of his associates enters the room with a flask of what Rene assumes is water. He throws his arm into the liquid which was actually lavender essence. Almost immediately his burning decreased. Then, with repeated applications, the burn healed completely without a trace of scar. In 1920 Mr. Gattefosse coined the phrase *aromatherapie*. While this may be the first use of a word to describe the use of essential oils, the actual practice dates back to ancient Greeks, Romans, Arabs, Egyptians.

Lemon

The common lemon was not always so common. The lemon began its worldly route in China. Arabian merchants may have brought it to the Mediterranean as mosaics at Pompeii show images of a fruit that looks like a lemon. Certainly the lemon was available during the Cursades. The earliest record of the lemon in the New World came from Haiti and the Dominican Republic, where it arrived with Columbus in 1493. You have heard the

CREATE BEAUTIFUL RELATIONSHIPS 4

At six in the morning the sun spreads its wings over the evergreen trees that wall the slopes surrounding Shambhala's Great Stupa of Dharmakaya, an expression of the aspiration for peace, harmony and equanimity for all beings. The light has not yet touched the Stupa. The oldest form of Buddhist architecture, a Stupa can best be described as a living spiritual monument. To a child it appears as a delicious layer-cake decorated with colorful ornaments and golden candles. Around the globe, Stupas are symbols of the enlightened mind, the awakened mind, as well as the path for this realization. The structure represents the Buddha's body, speech and mind. Every part is carefully tailored with symbolism and sacred geometry to show the path towards enlightenment. Today the Dalai Lama comes to bless the Stupa and receive a Living Peace Award from Sakyong Mipham Rinpoche, the Shambhala linage holder.

It is the middle of September and the weather is unusually cold. For two days we have practiced meditation in a large tent draped in fresh snow. It is the only time I have meditated wearing a winter parka and long johns. In an odd way I find it the perfect environment for meditation because it challenges me to let go of my perceptions about my physical body and how it feels. Today I wake up at five, excited about the prospect of seeing His Holiness and participating in the ceremonies.

When I get to the seating area it is still quite early. There are more than two thousand metal chairs set up. In the first row that rings the front of the Stupa there is one seat left. It is off to the far right side at an awkward angle behind the stage. A man in a wheelchair sits at the end. It is not what I wanted because I won't be able to see the Dalai Lama very well. But, since it's in the front, I decide to park myself here. About two hours later the beating of helicopter blades grows louder than the wind. His Holiness arrives.

A number of monks walk over to greet the Dalai Lama as his car drives up towards the Stupa. I suddenly realize that this entourage will actually walk right past me on the way to the stage. I scoop my digital camera out of my jacket pocket to get some pictures. As they approach I recognize the Dalai Lama from the thousands of pictures I've seen.

He is wearing his traditional layered robes, yellow over red. His right arm is fully exposed from the shoulder down. Suddenly he stops, directly in front of me. He leans down to touch the man in the wheelchair and say a few words. He straightens up, looks directly at me and says quietly, "It is cold here." Suddenly, I have the best seat.

His Holiness delivers a speech that resonates with Buddhist teachings, but also with his trademark focus on compassion and peace. He speaks slowly, thoughtfully. "Most important is peace of mind which comes from compassion. Unbiased compassion. Everyone has the seed of compassion. It is important to nurture this seed. All different traditions. Like ancient Hinduism, Buddhism, Judaism, Christainity, Islam, and so on, in spite of different philosophies the real message is the same: A message of Love, Compassion, Forgiveness, Tolerance, Contentment."

He goes on to explain, "Form is emptiness and emptiness is form. Not that nothing exists; but things exist in their dependent nature. Our hands, the wind. There are many possibilities. One is that when they are combined we feel cold. In our naive experience we think of our hands, and the wind as being independent objects."

It is incredible. Like all great teachers His Holiness can take the circumstances of the moment and weave them into the teachings. Little did I imagine when he shared with me his feeling about the temperature that it would become part of his message. He shares that interconnectedness and interdependency have three levels. One is changing phenomena that are momentary. Like our hands and the wind at this particular moment. A second is unchanging phenomena. The Tathagata-garbha sutra or doctrine describes the Buddha nature as the essence or Self of all beings, including both the Buddha and everyone else. This essence is immortal, unchanging, and the cause of Buddhahood. A third phenomena is something that does not exist in its own right.

With a few sentences the Dalai Lami explains the essential aspect of not only the human condition; but also the key elements that tie us together. Further, he details the processes that ensure harmony and peace on both an individual and global level. Put simply, if we focus on bringing love, compassion, forgiveness, tolerance and contentment into our lives we are golden. To do this effectively we need to recognize the coexistence, interconnectedness and interdependency between ourselves and others.

What counts is the relationship you are having with yourself, and with others, at any one moment. This is a puzzle with two pieces. You are one piece. Everyone else is the other piece. When the pieces come together magic happens. It is through our interaction with others that we give and receive meaning for our own lives.

Co-Creation: Work With Others to Realize A Dream

The manifestation and the success of any dream you have, depends upon the engagement and interaction of others. Frequently we take our ideas, our seeds, and pass them onto others. This can be done in the spirit of sharing or the spirit of co-creation. Sharing is when you freely give your ideas and input to someone else because you know they may be able to give birth where you cannot. You are literally moving a seed to more fertile territory.

Co-creation is different. With co-creation you are either going to ask others to help you birth your ideas; or you are going to help them birth theirs. Done well, co-creation is action that acknowledges and employs the positive aspects of our interdependence with others. Co-creation is essential if a thought form is going to move into the physical world. We can do many things by ourselves; but in almost every instance it requires the assistance of others to realize our dreams. You can sit in a closet and design a building; write a book or a song; envision world peace. That may be the end of it, which is perfectly o.k. When a creation of this nature is discussed, constructed, published, recorded, distributed, enacted and ultimately enjoyed by other people; the magic of our ability to co-create occurs.

Co-creation occurs in many forms. Sometimes we inspire others to join in and "play with us." This type of co-creation provides the best examples of leadership and success because the outcome, the manifestation of the dream, is jointly shared and jointly created. When you don't have to win or compete with anyone the journey is fun. We also have to be comfortable and enjoy helping others with their birthing process. In both instances we need to remember the relationship and potential problems that occur if we begin co-creation glued to a specific outcome. Success blossoms from engagement in the process of co-creation.

For success to occur, co-creation depends upon aligning your intention with the intention of the others who are creating with you. If two (or more) people co-create, but have not aligned their intentions, they will never manifest or create what they believe they have agreed on. The underlying issue is that people often agree on something verbally, but their intentions are not matched. It is like having several people in the same lifeboat, but paddling in different directions. The boat is either going in circles or going nowhere fast. Yet everyone wonders why.

Intention, whether it be for yourself, or for co-creators, is your direction. Your boat needs a direction or it will never reach land. *Attention* is how you (or the group) are going to focus your energy to realize the mutually agreed upon intention. You decide to head west. Are you going to row? Put up a sail? Start the engine?

Energy always follows attention. This is important, and it is true for the physical, mental and spiritual aspects of yourself; and it is true for anything you are trying to birth. Let me share something that seems obvious, but individuals and groups of people do it all the time. It takes more energy to be fragmented than it does to be focused. That is because each fragment requires energy to continue moving. Focused attention of energy with clear intention always creates results.

The easiest way to synchronize a team is the same way you do it for yourself. Simply check and discover if their intention matches yours. Let's spend a moment on conversation. Communication is a unique gift we all have. But communication can create clarity, or confusion. Listening, not talking, is the key. Deep Listening. Sometimes we say we are listening, or nod our head like we are in agreement, but we have not really heard a thing. So we have agreed without acknowledging what the other party is telling us. One way to fix this is to verbalize what you and the other parties believe is an agreement. Something as simple as, "What I heard you say is (blank). Is that correct? Are we in agreement?" This creates a verbal contract for a shared understanding and a common intention.

Usually the first thing that people want to talk about in any conversation is their intent at that moment. Become keenly aware of the initial part of every dialog. Not only what others say, but what you yourself say. I am having a Reiki session with Cindy, my incredible massage therapist and energy worker. Before we start she asks, "How is it going? What's happening in your life?" I tell her I have just made a big change and am starting something new (this book). It feels to me like jumping off a cliff. Cindy looks at me and says, "O.K. Let's see if we can transform **jumping off a cliff** into **flying off a mountaintop with new wings**."

It is not until I hear her verbalize what I had just said, until I hear my own words echoing back at me, that I realize importance of my words. I examine the mental image of jumping off a cliff. It is suicidal. Cindy is correct. I need to shift my own viewpoint towards one of flying to new horizons; not leaping to sudden death. Sometimes we need to have another voice feed us back our own viewpoint in order to recognize it, and formalize a proper intention.

Be expansive during every conversation, whether you are on the phone or in person. Everything that is said by anyone in attendance adds to the conversation. It is all related. If you are having a meeting, a discussion, about a project that you are seeding you need to be extremely open. Whether the dialog is between you and one other person, or a group of fifty, allow that aspect of you that created the seed to also recognize and include the spirit of the other individuals. Their contributions are essential to your success.

Stay true to the intention, and not to everyone's horizontal stories. People will take what you verbalize; they will interpret you with their personal filters, then immediately go off into *their* story about the situation. In fact other people are silently waiting to see if they will agree or disagree with you before you even say one word. It can be a challenge to stay with the intention.

As you talk with others watch to see if they "go off," wandering into their stories. You can recognize this easily as people have a tendency to have their eyes move away, usually up and to the left or right, when other thoughts come in. Recognize that other people are simply doing what they are doing. Be aware that sometimes we, and the people we expect action from, want to stay in the process. The reason is that we (or they) do not actually want to reach a final decision. The current moment provides the teaching; and it is the place for seeding and birthing.

Seeding and Birthing Projects

On a cosmic scale, creation and destruction are an endless process. Spirit transforms into substance and then moves back to spirit again. It never stops. If you understand the principles behind creation and destruction you have a better opportunity to manifest your dreams. Creation always comes about from the interaction between male and female energies. Conceiving and giving birth to a child is the most obvious and profound example of human creation. The result is more profound than any other act of human creation. The birth of any baby born far exceeds the greatest architecture, literature or work of science.

While male and female do refer to man and woman, they also refer to the male and female energies which reside in all of us. It is the yin and the yang, the Chinese principles which describe how what seem to be opposing forces are actually bound together and intertwined creating everything in the natural world. Male energy is the seed of creation, of ideas. Female energy gives birth.

How then, in everyday life, can you use this principle to achieve the manifestation of your dreams? The seeds of creation appear as ideas, sometimes when you are awake and sometimes in your dreams. Then the game begins. The seed has been planted, either through inspiration or because someone else handed it over. Now it has to grow with actions.

There are two aspects of seeding that can help move the process forward. One aspect is this: knowing that the seed has been planted and it is time to wait. Frequently in life, and in business, we show impatience. It is a particularly bad characteristic in the United States and parts of Europe where people have come to expect instantaneous results for every action. Send an email. If you don't get a reply within ten minutes you wonder if there is a problem.

Not all plants grow to maturity in eight hours. As soon as you have passed an idea, a request, a proposal, anything over to another person for their consideration the seed is in the ground. If you call them back too soon it simply does no good. It is like telling a little seed "grow faster." It can not. You actually start to overwater the seed and potentially kill it before it sprouts.

From a business and personal perspective you are hitting your head on a brick wall, frustrating yourself and the other parties to whom you are requesting a response or commitment faster than they are willing to do so. The female aspect of the birthing process requires that everything needs a certain amount of time to come forth. Learn how to let it happen. Do not force it. Dreams come in repetitive patterns at different times. The universe is asking you to unlock the form.

Each person will birth in their own time and no faster. You can not speed up their delivery. What you can do, however, is plant seeds in multiple locations. If you have an idea that can go out, or be seeded, with multiple parties simultaneously then do so. If you wait for the birthing aspect of creation you will get better results. A more appropriate time, complete with all of the right circumstances for your success, may be right around the corner.

Secrets to Achieve Movement – Fixed and Free Dancing

I am hiking in Rattlesnake Canyon, an extremely remote part of the Colorado National Monument. It is late afternoon. Rain suddenly appears, falling down in sheets. What I don't realize is that the red clay dirt which is the foundation of the four-wheel drive road is turning into a slippery, yet glue-like substance that prevents my Ford Bronco II from moving. I am stuck. My tent sits twenty miles away. I sleep in the car, occasionally turning on the engine for a little warm air. In the morning the sun arrives, dries up the soil; and I am gone.

There are times in life that things seem to get stuck in the proverbial mud. No matter how hard you try you can not get traction. Why? And what can you do?

> ➢ Open yourself to the possibility of more than one outcome.
> ➢ Establish a clear intention.
> ➢ If you co-create make sure everyone on the team shares the same intention.
> ➢ Ensure you proceed and act with a spirit of abundance.
> ➢ Allow enough time for the project to birth.

You might need to get moving again. You have direction, you know where you are going, but the wheels are spinning. You may need to shift your approach. There are two types of approaches to every situation.

One is called a fixed dance. The other is a free dance. Just as the names suggest, one approach is well defined; the other is quite loose. Both approaches work; and sometimes you need to integrate both to achieve success.

Consider salsa dancing. Latin-based, salsa has a pattern of six steps danced over eight counts of music. Salsa dancers move side-to-side and integrate turns. The foundation is fixed. Get out on a dance floor and salsa becomes unique to every couple. Variations on the basics are endless. Dancers free flow on top of the fixed pattern. For soccer fans the analogy is similar. The game always has eleven players who play against eleven other players. This is fixed. The moment the soccer ball is in play the game becomes a free flow where everyone instantly goes with the free flow, reacting to circumstances that change rapidly.

Now, imagine a line on the floor directly in front of you. Make it five feet wide. On one side of this line there is a little sign that says "I need to be in control." At the other end is a little sign that says "I go completely with the flow." Go stand on the line at the point that best describes yourself in most situations. The two ends of this spectrum are similar to the fixed and free dance. If you are "stuck" with something in life - realizing an intention, a project, a relationship, a health issue – you need to move to a different point on the spectrum. You may need to move closer to the fixed or the free dance to achieve forward movement.

If the wheels of your carefully orchestrated plan are not turning, move towards a free dance. This may require shelving the current plan entirely and brainstorming twenty new plans as a means to re-evaluating the first plan. This does not mean you have to erase the board and start over. Just see if there is uncharted territory that can be explored. If you are co-creating, get input from your partners.

If your co-creator is your spouse, or significant other, you may need to find an entirely new space to play in. The reason is that you have both fixed your viewpoint and have a hard time wavering from it. This is not about having your spouse or significant other move to accept your idea. It is about both of you moving on the spectrum. Find a fresh perspective. Dance it for a little while to see if the energy picks up.

Since opposites are part of yin and yang, the opposite can also be true. You may be stuck because you *are* free dancing too much. You are all over the place. You have an endless list of great ideas and directions. You can't stand still. It looks and feels like a lot is happening. But this is not move-ment. You are like wheels spinning in mud. There is a lot of energy, but little forward direction. For you, moving towards a fixed dance may infuse new forward movement to your intention. A fixed dance can be a daily routine that you get into. Or, narrow down your list of twenty great ideas to the top two and focus attention on them.

Just like salsa dancers or baseball players you can combine fixed and free dancing. For example, you need to plan a meeting. If you make an appointment, schedule the meeting for a specific date and time. That is now fixed. The people in attendance may be fixed. When the meeting begins allow yourself to free flow the dance while keeping your intentions in place. Free dance the agenda.

Relationships are a Vehicle for Transformation

To this point we have examined life in the context of co-creation. This is an important area because we spend a large portion of our life in a work environment where, in essence, we are seeding and birthing ideas. Let's examine relationships with their complex interdependencies using a dif-ferent lens. Generally you can organize your relationships into the follow-ing categories: work and business, friends, family, intimate and teacher/ student.

Each of these relationships represents a vehicle. They are unique learning environments for your personal transformation. Each vehicle ex-ists within a specific period of time. Some relationships last for only five minutes and others last a lifetime.

Each carries its own unique set teachings. Without placing any judg-ment on the nature of the relationships (good or bad) you need to un-derstand the opportunity for personal learning and transformation. That is what every relationship is about. It is your chance to see how you experience the love, compassion, forgiveness, tolerance and contentment that the Dalai Lama speaks about. What is your experience of these active human qualities in both directions? What comes to you, *and* what do you present to others. And, what is the relationship between the two?

You can both intuitively and analytically examine what is happening within different relationships in several ways. The most important is this very moment. Watch what is happening as it happens. This is the best opportunity to have a transformative experience because you can simultaneously monitor yourself in an interaction that carries a built-in habitual pattern; and stop to create a new pattern. For example, you have a family member that always complains about their health. You always try to change the subject because it is sooooo boring. The moment you recognize a relationship-oriented pattern that you are actively involved in is the time you make a shift.

The other way to look at what is happening is with a perspective of time. Today what has happened in terms of your relationships? Were you consistent? Were you compassionate at home and indifferent at work? Were you indifferent at home but compassionate at work? What created the difference? If you look at a longer time frame what patterns arise? Have you had six relationships that all began or ended the same way?

Do not judge yourself, or others. The exercise is to identify patterns that occur in your life. When you recognize a pattern you can decide if you like it; or if it no longer serves as a tool for personal growth.

One of the unique ways the universe works is that it delivers directly to our doorstep the situations and the relationships we need for growth. Kind of like karmic home delivery. If we use relationships and the lessons that are tied directly to them for growth we can move ahead. However, if we move ahead without learning, the universe conspires to give us a new opportunity that is exactly what we already had. In other words, we did not learn.

This is why so much of the spiritual path is about self inquiry. Not only are you the one and only person that can change the interactions within any of your containers; you are also the only person that can judge whether you have learned. Your friends and family have their ideas about your situation(s); but they are not in your skin.

The key is consciousness. If movement and change align with your intention, which is connected to your spirit, you will be happy. If movement is driven by ego you will find yourself back where you started. You are the only person that really knows the answer to this aspect of transformation.

The Special Relationship of Parents and Children

Through all the years of our life there are two unique sets of relationships. The relationship we have with our parents - and the relationship with our children. These relationships usually last longer than any other relationship.

In many cases it is a connection that carries through most of our life. The length of these relationships is one unique characteristic. Just think of all the lessons we receive from parents and children over our lifetime.

Second, it is unlikely that you will abandon your parents or your children. Your job sucks, and you quit. You may never communicate with any of your co-workers again. Interestingly, companies and organizations are composed of a group of individuals who all experience a collective relationship in a container referred to as "the company." Just like a person, when an organizational container is filled with expectations, ego and fear, the organization cannot realize forward movement or success.

You select and change your relationships with friends, co-workers and significant others at your discretion. It can happen in a heartbeat. Parents give you the precious gift of birth; take time to raise, educate and support you. Regardless of what you believe or feel, an intimate bond exists. One of the reasons parent/child relationships are close is because they provide extensive teachings.

Few people take these relationships lightly because they encompass such a potent mixture of teachings, roles and emotions including compassion, responsibility, commitment, surrender, joy and pride. Unconditional love is one of the best teachings you receive and give in these roles. There may be times, short or long, when events in this distinctive relationship do not provide a Hollywood Movie ending. That can offer teaching as well. You may disassociate, even disown, your parents or your children. The teachings remain intact.

Nurture, Nature and Predestination

There is a common saying, "We can not choose our parents (or children)." About the closest we have come with modern science is using MicroSort®, a method created by Genetics & IVF Institute of Virginia U.S.A. that separates the male sperm from the female, to help pre-select the sex of newborns. The rest, it seems, is up to chance. It appears that from our first breath we somewhat randomly get a good deal or we don't.

There is a different theory, with variations, offered by many religions. This theory states that where you come into life is, in fact, carefully predetermined by the universe, God, Allah. For many people, as years move on and seemingly unexplainable events occur, this may leave a lot of unanswered questions. It has a tendency to separate you, the individual spirit, from a master plan that is so large it is difficult to grasp.

There is another idea; one that I have come to embrace. As a spiritual being, your own spirit negotiates with the universe prior to birth or incarnation. This is not a standard business negotiation. "Universe, if you allow me to be born to those rich Hollywood actors I promise to do everything I can to save the endangered Banded Hare Wallaby."

Which life is going to best serve you? Provide experiences and teachings that your soul needs. There is actually no way that our mind, or at least the left hemisphere of our brain, can ever understand what this pre-incarnation process is like. It is said the soul hovers around the mother before the connection is made between soul and body. Before your spirit incarnates it negotiates what lessons you need in this lifetime. There are different opinions about when the soul actually comes into the physical body. It is usually not at conception, but sometime later. As late, according to the teachings of Shri Dhyanyogi Madhusudandasji, as the fifth month of pregnancy.

This timing may be of great concern, and debate, with individuals who want to present their case for or against abortion. This timing is irrelevant for teachings about the relationship between parents and children. What is relevant is that you have taken part in the process that drives many of the teachings you have an opportunity to participate in. This perspective has the potential to place an entirely new light on your understanding, and judgment, of the experiences of your life.

It suggests is that everything that comes your way is part of a larger plan. However, it is not a predetermined plan! It is simply a unique and personal gateway for your own transformation. The universe does not write the script for every little thing that your parents or children will do. And, it does not determine your response. This is free will. You are simply provided the very best container for your life that can be imagined.

This is the point where it is easy to create stories. Why would anyone choose to be born with a handicap? Why would the universe let someone like Hitler be born when some angelic child dies as a baby? We create stories; and then we judge the stories we create. It is difficult to accept that we cannot comprehend the mystery. We are connected to the universe and to God. But we ourselves are not the entire universe or God.

Perhaps a baby dies after six short months because they have learned the lesson they came here for. Maybe the grief the parents endure unlocks a door of compassion that they both came to learn. We do not need to know the answer. The story is extraneous. Just as any stories of past lives can be irrelevant.

I did not say they were incorrect. A story can be told with great accuracy. Just like reading a history book. But, like history, there can be a lot of different interpretations about events. If we get stuck in a story we build a brick wall that prevents transformation. What we need to do is accept every situation that comes to us as a personal teaching lovingly prepared and served directly by the universe. What journey could possibly be more perfect than your own? No one else on this planet has a better life for you. This Buddhist prayer details what we all desire.

May all beings be happy.
May all beings be free from pain and suffering.
May all beings be free from sickness and disease.
May all beings be free from attachment and affliction.
May all beings be free from danger and delusion.
May all beings be filled with loving kindness and compassion.
May all beings attain Nirvana.

Become Free From Attachment

May all beings be free from attachment. Stories and attachment go hand in hand. So, what causes storytelling? How can we stop it? And are there any benefits?

Everything, except this very moment, is a story. Stories become an integral part of who we are. Teachings and transformation are intimately connected to the story that creates them. Stories are such a critical aspect of growth and transformation that storytelling goes beyond personal experience. From early childhood we are told bedtime stories. Over the course of our life, we absorb the stories contained and shared in thousands of books, television programs, movies, the Internet. And, we dream. We are literally asleep thirty percent of our life (that's if you sleep 8 hours a night); and about half of that is engaged in dreaming. According to an article published on the School of Metaphysics web site[3] by age 60 the average person will dream 87,000 hours and have approximately

---

3   Why Do We Dream 1996 Vol. 14 No. 1

197,100 dreams. That is a lot of stories (and teachings) that you may or may not remember.

Everything that is important about a story, the experience, growth, sharing, compassion, love, occurs as the story unfolds. The story itself is a blessing. And for this aspect, every story has an incredible power that can be shared and revisited. *Goldilocks and the Three Bears.* The time you saved the stray cat by stuffing it in your jacket and sneaking it into your bedroom.

We can hear and tell great stories a hundred times. Each time we may appreciate a new facet, even recognize a new lesson. That is the upside of a story. The downside is that a repetitive mental story creates a framework about our conception of ourselves and others. If this happens, the story becomes an attachment which prevents forward movement, and the ability to create new stories.

Living in the moment, in the present, is the foundation of many eastern philosophies. It is core to the practice of yoga. We recognize that the past is gone. The future has not happened yet. Yet we spend an enormous percentage of our life in those places. It's like we have a little time machine inside our head that loves to move back and forth. Let me review what happened yesterday. Again. Complete with mental actors the dialog recurs, just like a movie. What will I be doing tomorrow? Where do you see yourself in five years? How will it be different than yesterday?

In the worst case scenario, the mind morphs stories into opium-like reveries where an individual becomes lost in thought. Or, in the case of post-traumatic stress disorder, anxiety and reactions derived from an extremely traumatic event become haunting long after the event is over.

The reason we lock into stories is because the moment anything happens we get a story. It writes itself. Here is where it is easy to make a mistake. We believe that every story can, or will, be repeated. Especially very good, or bad stories. Imagine you are a child (or adult) taking a walk in a park. Unexpectedly a dog runs up and bites your leg. You will probably be nervous every time you see a dog running your way. But, you could also be incorrect the next four hundred times.

Three men are walking together in a dark ally at midnight. One of the men sees a large snake and yells, "SNAKE." A second man with a serious heart condition has a heart attack and dies on the spot. The third man walks up to the snake and discovers that it is not a deadly cobra. It is only a coiled rope. Well, it is too late for the man who was afraid of snakes. His story killed him. Our mind is the carrier of time-bound memories. Not only the memories of what has happened to us before; but also the previous conclusions.

Part of the challenge is to not lock into any story as being unavoidably repeatable. This is hard. It requires fresh, child eyes all the time. One beautiful aspect of being "born again" is that everything comes at you fresh, without history or story. The future is infinite in the present moment if you accept the present moment again and again as it is. A challenge is that stories feed our ego. It does not matter if the story is incredibly good, or fantastically bad. Either way our ego takes detailed notes, and creates a pattern that becomes an aspect of own self identity.

Events we live through allow our ego to create a story about ourselves. Like a snowball that tumbles down a mountainside and gathers so much force it creates an avalanche, these personal stories begin to assume history and power. I am a fantastic lover. I am not confident in front of large crowds. I am beautiful. I am ugly. The process of ego identification, which happens for everyone, tightly wraps these stories around the perception we have of our self. We identify our self with the story, but not with the learning or transformative experience. This process turns us into an object in the story, as opposed to a living spirit that can change, transform, grow and become whatever we want. As a result we relive the same story many times. This is *Goldilocks* gone bad.

Because we craft our own story so well - both in the past and the future - other people, *especially* our parents and children collaborate our story and reinforce our world view. "Yes, you are a great lover." "You really are not good at public speaking." We expect nothing less then the story; and we are stuck. The CD or the MP3 plays the same song even when we say we do not like what we are hearing.

Think of all the rituals we go through to keep the stories alive. Like a drug addict who has to steal a TV Set to sell it to get money to find a drug dealer to buy their drug to shoot up. All the time they believe the drug is their addiction. The entire story is their addiction.

Why does our ego do this? It is hard to believe it is our ego. Why doesn't it work for us? Often, our ego jumps in to protect us from being hurt. It does this no matter which way the coin lands. Either those other people are "right about me", or they are "the biggest jerks." Unfortunately our ego-protector is doing this in a way that enhances what hurt us in the first place. Transformation in any relationship, with any group of people, can only occur when you recognize the story as a story. You must stop and change it in the present moment. The process of intention setting can help with this.

Do not forget that you have a bi-directional role in every story. Just as you want to transform the story that is about you; you need to transform your stories about other people. Your lover, brother-in-law, employee has an annoying habit. You know they are going to act that way the next time you see them. You nail them before they even walk in the door. STOP. Even if they come in and it seems like the annoying habit is coming. Recognize the power that you have to shift the entire relationship by not buying into the story. You help *them* transform!

Now, Thank Your Ego

Enough with ego bashing. A large percentage of spiritual seekers view the ego as an ugly little monster that needs to be confined in a high security vault, or completely annihilated. Neither is correct. Our ego plays an incredibly valuable role in self development. It is the foundation for many of our actions. Actions (karma is actions and deeds) create the samskaras (the tendencies to do certain things) which provide a series of ongoing lessons.

The ego is essential to our ability to learn and grow. The dance we want to learn is how to use consciousness to step back from the ego when we find ourselves in reaction. Learn to be witness to actions rather than an unwilling participant. To acknowledge what is happening and say, "Thank you for showing me this about myself. It is an area that needs further investigation." Do not fight your ego. You will never win. Rather, see it as a fantastic tool, a partner in your self development. Even when it takes over completely it is o.k. Maybe you really need that lesson one more time. You can't learn to Tango in a week even if you dance with the stars. This dance takes a lot of practice.

Learn to Live In the Present

It is common practice to make an enemy out of the present; and a friend with the future. We have been training for years. Things will be better when _____ (fill in the blank) happens. I will be happy when I achieve

_____ (fill in the blank). It is commonplace to be possessed by memories of the past. Memories that define who you are; how you act and what you can achieve.

From about age two humans begin to be affected by the forces of attraction and repulsion. You like something, or you don't like something. Obviously we want more of what we like and less of what we don't like. Over time these predispositions become ingrained not only as memories, but as active forces in decision making and judgment. In other words, your likes and dislikes become habitual patterns. These habits layer over your energy body. Whenever you experience a reaction you are completely out of touch with what is happening in the moment. By the time we reach the age of thirty, if we are not highly conscious, instead of living our life we begin to live our habits.

How do you return to the present moment? When all of your fragmented forces are brought to play on the present, you, the performer, disappear. The word _persona_ describes the large masks that early Greek actors would use to portray characters. Outdoor amphitheaters were so large that nuances of a performance could be lost without these oversized masks, which offered information about the personality of the character.

In modern psychology the term persona still applies to the mask that we wear in various social settings. To live fully in the present you need to drop all of your masks. Like meditation, this can not be achieved with will power or thinking. You must become the performance; moving in perfect harmony with the story as it unfolds.

There is a timeless state of joy in the moment. The joy comes from you. The trap to avoid is not to become addicted with attraction to the person or event that provides this feeling. Because they don't provide it. You do. The external source is not your joy. Learn how to tune into the power inside you that creates your life and happiness in the present moment. Do not identify with your time-body. Every reaction comes from your time-body which are memories (the past) and projections (the future).

The Storytellers: Attraction and Repulsion

By understanding why and how we get stuck in a story, we give ourselves tools and opportunities to use every story productively. A productive use of a story is as a tool for transformation; or to move us towards a desired intention.

Stories begin when we have an attraction to, or repulsion of, a person, place, event, experience. At that moment the story begins. Sit in a circle surrounded by twenty complete strangers. As your eyes move around the circle there will be people you are immediately attracted to; and others you would not want to sit next to.

On the surface you may think it is just their physical appearance that attracts or repels you. It is much more. There is a magnetic attraction or repulsion set up between you and this other person. Remember, you do not even know them. In almost every case when you have a strong attraction or repulsion (person, place, experience, etc.) this indicates that you have a transformative lesson sitting right in front of you.

If you play with magnets you know that when North and South poles face against each other, the magnets want to snap together. When like poles face each other you can not force them to touch. It is similar with people. When the magnetic is attraction, the person supports your current energy. Not because they are identical to you; but rather because they support you. They keep your energy going and you feel good in their presence.

As Plato notes, "Friends have all things in common." That is why we like our friends so much. This unique relationship means our friends support us, and our belief systems. Great friends step over this line. They tell you when they disagree with you. Even when they believe you are moving your life in an unhealthy direction. You know these are great friends because they are willing to risk the friendship in the spirit of friendship.

The natural flow of attraction and repulsion, positive and negative polarity, creates harmony in life. Just as the flow of energy of the greatest magnet, planet Earth, keeps the planet in harmony. Balance is created by the natural rhythm of polarity. Trouble begins at a personal level when you choose positive or negative, attraction or repulsion. As soon as you choose one of the two options you start to create an obsession, possibly an addiction to a state of experience. And, you create a fear of either not having it, or of receiving it. The most powerful example is when you fall in love with another person.

Love, Attraction and Repulsion in Relationships

Being in love is fantastic. When you are in love you surrender yourself completely and are happy when the other person is happy. This is true love. But even love comes with variations that over time begin to look like attraction and repulsion. What happens when the person you love doesn't want to see you anymore? Your attraction, which you now mistake for love, suddenly becomes a problem.

Imagine you are sitting in the living room reading a book. Your spouse or significant other walks in the room and declares with a smile, "I am leaving tomorrow morning. I am going to Peru to fulfill my life dream of owning a potato farm." Remember that true love where your only desire was *their* happiness? If this still held, you would look at them, smile, and say, "Wow, that is fantastic! I will stay here and take care of the children. Would you like to bring the gardening tools?"

That is not what most people do. A more common response would be, "WHAT? Have you lost your mind? What am I going to do?" Suddenly the story is all about you. Love is now attachment with a side dish of fear. You need to disengage from both the attachment and the fear.

It is significantly easier when people who repulse us don't want to play. In the back of your mind there's a little story running that says, "Please move away from me." But these individuals can be our best teachers. Just like magnets, the most common reason that someone has a quality that you do not appreciate is because it resonates within you. The two south poles don't want to touch. In fact they are a mirror for you. You see something you do not like in them because you recognize it in yourself. They are showing you this quality. A quality you have present, or one that is just below the surface.

The value of recognizing and learning from mirrors that other people provide us is immeasurable. Literally everyone is your teacher. Those unique individuals who energetically grab your attention are the best teachers. You may know them for years, or only few minutes. There is something that attracts or repels you. No one else will have exactly the same reaction that you do to this person.

Watch your reaction carefully. Step back from the reaction to notice the quality of the behavior that attracts or repels you. Either way, know with certainty that you have this same quality. Possibly this person sees it in you in exactly the same way that you see it in them. The value of having an emotionally detached view of the mirror is that you can more clearly see yourself. Because it is always easier to see what is happening, especially psychological tendencies, when you look at someone else. Simply take the knowledge that you get from compassionate viewing and apply this to both your own growth and to your interaction with the other person. This is not a big winded process. Remember, you may only be with this teacher for a few minutes. Learn and apply your wisdom immediately.

Understand Your Reactions

Our personal attractions and repulsions are derived from a lifetime (or lifetimes) of repetitive stories. If we understand that we have artificially created attractions and repulsions we can begin to understand how to transform a story as it occurs. Let's examine what happens.

A magnetic field begins an attraction or repulsion to a person, place, or experience. This attraction or repulsion occurs because we ourselves have a certain magnetic field. The fields are created by our own past experiences and stories which give power to and reinforce them. We want to repeat being with people and having experiences we like; and avoid people and experiences we do not enjoy.

There is another aspect to the magnetism of relationships which plays out frequently. Because opposites attract it is common to find people with opposite personality traits together in relationships. There is a natural attraction. Depending upon the specifics of the relationship this dichotomy can be healthy - or not. Because of the strong magnetism it can be challenging for individuals to acknowledge their specific role in the relationship.

A caregiver is in a relationship with someone who needs care. A person who enjoys control is in a relationship with someone who has fears and self doubts. A risk taker who doesn't mind chaos in life is involved with someone who enjoys stability and control. Introverts with extroverts. Does it ring any bells? I do not want to imply that you need to change. Everything happens for a reason. I do believe that awareness of your role and the energetic magnetism involved can provide liberation. The acknowledgement of who you are, why you have the relationships you do, and what the teachings are, will open doors for personal discovery and growth.

Remember how the universe uses opposites? When we make a choice, we create an energy that guarantees we will also encounter the opposite. The Earth itself is currently shifting it's poles. South is destined to become magnetic North. All human experiences contain the potential for opposites. What great Masters understand is that effortless happiness – Nirvana - comes through learning how to not choose. In other words, every person, event and experience in your life is viewed as "good" without exception, attraction or repulsion.

In addition to attraction and repulsion, once you start to judge yourself in relation to other people, you are in for trouble. There are only two choices. Either you are better than they are, or you are not good enough. As soon as you choose, use your ego, you rely on your personal conditioning and history to make a decision. Do not make the choice. Simply do not choose that one is better than another. You or them. This is what creates separation from others.

One attribute of every pre-programmed attraction or repulsion is that you immediately want to control it. When it is under your control you are safe and can ensure your reaction. Let's consider extreme cases. In an extreme case of attraction the only way you can control the person, place, thing or event is to own it. It is not currently legal to own another person; but you certainly can control people. The object of your attraction (lover, employee, pet, house) is put under obligation to comply with your desires. As a result, your reaction is guaranteed. You are satisfied that they are doing what you want them to do.

In an extreme case of repulsion you don't want the person, place, thing, event to exist. You would like to annihilate it. You have a significant fear of spiders. Every time you see a spider you reach for a newspaper to whack it out of existence. Its death ensures the reaction you want. In this case you don't have to have any further reactions. Ironically, spiders would be the worst animal to kill if you are trying to change your life. As an animal totem, spiders represent creativity and the weaving of fate. Spiders teach that what you do in the present helps determine your future.

Paradoxically, the moment you place attachment on a person, item or event; it possesses you. If I told you that my uncle Joe Smith's car was stolen this morning you might think, feel and say, "Oh, that's too bad." However, if I told you that your car was just stolen your reaction would be considerably different. Clearly, neither ownership nor oblivion of objects you desire or distaste will solve the core issue. **Your reaction**. It is never what someone else does to you that actually bothers you. Rather, it is what you do with it.

The universal law of Attraction brings you the circumstances, events, people that reflect who you are. A weather bell of who you are at any moment in time is demonstrated by your reactions. What is happening to you is what you are doing to yourself. You bring it in. This is the free-will puzzle piece that puts a significant element of responsibility on your shoulders. No longer can you blame anyone else for what is happening.

When things are going great we pay much less attention to this concept. You're in a great relationship; your parents and children love you; the economy and stock market are soaring; your car gets sixty miles to the gallon. Usually it's when the going gets tough that we get going with our reactions. So and so did this and that. Where did the money go? These are the times that we individually, and collectively, get crazy. Emotions flare, running the gamut from anger to depression, as we have our own uncontrolled reactions to circumstances that are also out of our control.

Remember the ego. When chaos abounds, in relationships or external events, the ego does not serve us well. In trying to protect us, it creates even more stories with accompanying reactions that further separate us from who we really are – a divine spirit.

Relationships. Important? Absolutely. Problems? No. Ego-based reactions are the problem. Reactions that are out of tune with who we really are, create disharmony in our relationships, finances and health. Conflict occurs when you say or think: "What I want is different than what is happening right now." The ego seeks safety, while the soul wants to be one with the divine.

How to Move Into Harmony with Relationships

In western music, harmony is defined as the structure of music with respect to its composition and the use and progression of chords. It is derived from the word "harmonic" which signifies related wavelengths of sound. The study of harmony, of harmonic progressions, concerns the movement from one pitch simultaneously to another, and the underlying principles that govern these progressions.

In life, as in music, we want to create harmonic progressions where our unique set of wavelengths resonate with circumstances, people and events. Composers, musicians, orchestras use scores or sheet music to play a work. Beethoven's Symphony No. 3 in E flat major has four movements that take about forty-five minutes to perform. Your life is considerably longer. What is important is that both musicians and the audience enjoy the music at just one place in the composition. That place is the present moment. You can only be listening to music, with it's intricate harmonics, right now. So too, the only place that you can create and adjust the harmony in your life is this moment.

The current moment offers a unique opportunity to simultaneously engage with others; create a story; view thoughts, reactions and actions in motion, and realize intention. This may seem like a lot to accomplish in a split second. If you can multitask driving a 4,000 pound SUV at seventy miles per hour, watch traffic, read billboards, drink a latte, listen to your iPod and have a conversation on your cell phone; then you simply need to practice being present in the moment.

People are like fruit trees. The seeds we have are our thoughts and our emotions. Ideally these would always reflect loving kindness. The fruits we offer are the words that we speak to other people. They come directly from our thoughts and emotions. Watch and see how incredibly fast a thought in your mind becomes a sentence poised for delivery. Observe how an emotional reaction moves like lightning from your solar plexus to your lips.

These fruits, our words, grow to become our physical actions. Clearly we need to watch the seeds themselves because they become what we do, and who we are. Spend time practicing consciousness, become aware at the genesis, the inception of your thoughts and emotions. This is the place to catch yourself in reaction. It can be too late by the time you say or do something you regret.

Loving kindness begets loving kindness. Violence begets violence. Many people have planted thoughts about you. You may have planted thoughts about yourself. You are not these images. They are a fiction. You are only spirit. You must give out exactly what you seek from others. Give acceptance. Give love. Give excitement and passion. Whatever you give from your heart, you receive this back.

The best technique is to work with your heart. Give up your heart; and when success comes don't presume that people are in love with your form, your name or your ego. Recognize that your soul made an expression, and you allow other people to express their soul. Each of us is a participant in an orchestra of people who are each unique, but also in harmony.

Talking Sticks and Circles Create Honest Dialog

Watching and catching yourself with a thought, or repetitive habit, in the moment can be helpful. It provides you the opportunity for almost instantaneous self reflection and transformation. Change can happen faster if both parties engage in the process.

EXERCISE

Deep Listening

The Talking Stick ensures that only one person at a time can speak. Unfortunately it does not ensure that all participants are listening to that person. If we accept being in "the moment" then our ears are totally open to the words and the energy of the person who is talking. But, like in any meeting, you can be present in a circle without listening. It is not uncommon for participants to mentally rehearse what they are going to say when it is their turn to have the talking stick. Obviously when this happens the amount of forward movement is limited because they have not heard the heart felt, energetic expressions of the other(s).

Listening is a tremendous skill. It is not only about being quiet. It is about giving your complete attention to all levels of communication. This includes not only the words, but feelings and other nonverbal messages. You can understand that if you are not quiet internally (i.e. mental chatter and preparation for your turn) that you really can not "hear" the other person. You are off on your story when you need to be present for them. It is in your best interest.

Deep Listening is a technique that empowers us to learn about each other and ourselves, as well as how we think. By learning to listen with a quiet and open mind it increases the opportunity for a group of two or more people to realize their mutual intentions. It facilitates spontaneous thinking and objectivity.

If appropriate you can do a Deep Listening exercise prior to using the Talking Stick because it helps make people more receptive to the dialog that occurs with Talking Stick. Get together with your partner, or group. If it is a group, create a circle. There are a few simple rules to follow for this exercise.

- All questions are open ended. Do not ask any questions that can have a "yes" or "no" answer.
- Do not ask a question that creates negative or defensive answers like, "Why do you dislike hot weather?"
- Every question should be spontaneous. The question you ask does not have to relate in any way to the previous question. But it can.
- Take only about one minute for your response.

Everyone starts with: "Hello, my name is _____, I do _____ and I am here to _____."

Then, the leader of this exercise begins: "My question for _____ (the person to his or her left) is, "_____?"

Questions can be broad, specific, universal, humorous or topical.

How do you feel infinite abundance can help each of us perform well for ourselves and this group?

What is your favorite color of clothing and why?

Complete the circle with this process and see what is learned.

Another technique for dissolving old, habitual patterns in close relationships, is to have an honest conversation with the person, or people you are having trouble with. This is not always easy. Here are a couple of useful ways to conduct conversations that open the door for new interactions and forward movement.

Talking stick. This ancient technique and custom of American Indian tribes is the foundation of a just and impartial discussion. It allows all members of a group to present their point of view with the sacred power of words. In council circles, the talking stick designates who has the right to speak. When a matter of importance comes before council, the leading elder holds the talking stick and begins discussion. When he or she finishes, they hold out the stick. Anyone that wants to speak now takes the stick. Everyone else must remain silent until the talking stick is passed on. In this manner the stick passes from one individual to another until all who wish to speak have done so.

The talking stick signifies open dialog. It assures the speaker they have the freedom and power to share from their heart. When you hold the talking stick you are allowed to use the sacred power of words. Talking stick ceremony creates absolute presence in the environment. Everyone focuses their undivided attention on the individual who is speaking. The energy in the room becomes both calm and focused on the words, the spirit, of one individual. In reality the talking stick is a Listening Stick.

Every aspect of a traditional Talking Stick carries symbolic meaning and power. The type of wood, ornaments, feathers, skins; they all bring significance and medicine to the ceremony. For example, Cedar symbolizes cleansing; White Pine is the tree of peace; Birch represents truth, Evergreen is growth; Aspen is a symbol for seeing clearly; Maple for gentleness; Elm represents wisdom; Mountain Ash is for protection; Oak stands for strength; Cherry has expression of love.

While traditionally crafted Talking Sticks carry great power; you can use any type of object for a ceremony of open discussion. Ideally the object has some element of nature. A stick, shell or feather. What is important is that when someone holds the object, only they are allowed to talk. The other(s) must remain quiet and listen. The person that asks for the discussion starts the ceremony. It is a good idea to begin with an honest overview that explains why you have asked to have a Talking Stick ceremony. Describe your intention.

In a large group begin by forming a circle. This is key. Because a circle has no beginning or end all participants carry equal weight in the discussion. A typical board room, with its long rectangular table, clearly puts the person at the head of the table at an elevated status. After the first person speaks, hand the stick to the person to your left when you are finished. Continue around the entire circle one time. Everyone in the group gets an opportunity to speak. If, after one full cycle, anyone wants to contribute again they may ask for the Talking Stick or object.

With two people let the Talking Stick move back and forth until both parties have said all they need to. It is o.k. if no conclusions are reached. Talking Stick ceremony is about the exchange of open dialog. The dialog will open up new movement in the relationship.

Talking Stick and Deep Listening are great ways to foster open communication with the intention of having participants learn about themselves and others they care about, while creating forward movement and shared intention. Like a frozen river, use these techniques to thaw the ice and allow waters that are flowing beneath the surface to break open movement on the surface.

Energy is in Every Relationship

A lot of references have been made to energy. Behind everything in the universe is energy. Einstein helped us understand that energy can never be destroyed... only changed in form. The first law of thermodynamics is known as the Law of Conservation of Energy. This law tells us that energy can be transferred from one system into another in many forms. And, energy can neither be created nor destroyed. As a result the total amount of energy available in the (known) universe is constant. Einstein's most famous equation describes the relationship between energy and matter:

$$E = mc2$$

In this equation, energy (E) is equal to matter (m) times the square of a constant (c). Einstein shows that energy and matter are interchangeable. Fortunately we do not need to be a physicist to understand the ramifications of this law.

It comes down to this. At the core everything is the same. Drop a couple of ice cubes into a pot on your stove and before long they turn to water, then evaporate as steam, which can again become water and ice.

Sunlight becomes photosynthesis in plants or electricity in solar panels. Seeds become plants which become food that humans and animals eat. A recording of music or voice to a CD which delivers energy to a speaker which we hear with our ears. Move your hand from shade into sunlight and feel the energy which, after a time, will burn your skin. This is physics in action.

All spiritual paths are about energy. In one respect, life is a series of energy transformers. There is Pure Matter. And there is Pure Energy with consciousness. When they are combined you have creation and existence. That is why, from a spiritual perspective, whatever we refer to with our personal lexicon as "god" must be worshipped both with and without form.

If everything has an energetic nature, then clearly our relationships, physical body, thoughts and emotions, health, finances all have an energetic element. This energy can be changed. Just like musicians can change the frequencies and harmonics in their music to impact the nature of the sound we hear; we can change the energy signature in our own bodies to create harmony. Many traditions, especially healing traditions, reference the energy within the human body. Words to name this energetic life force are known around the world. They include chi'i (pronounced "chee") in China, prana in India, ki in Japanese, mana in Hawaii; shakti in Sanskrit, and orenda in Native America.

Techniques for changing and using internal energy are the foundation of many healing systems including acupuncture, reflexology, Reiki, chakra healing and chemotherapy. It relates to the use of affirmations and mantras (sacred sounds and phrases) which create sounds that have energetic qualities that produce specific effects. Globally more than $20 billion annually is spent on the energy of radiation combined with chemotherapy as a treatment for cancer. Regardless of your philosophical or medicinal inclination, energy works.

Grounding Creates Stability

Roots. They provide both strength and self defense for every tree. Roots carry water and nutrients up into trees. Roots also perform the extremely valuable service of anchorage and food storage. Roots dive down into the earth. If trees did not have roots they would all fall over. Sometimes, as is the case with Cedar and Redwood tree, the root system is shallow. The roots of Giant Sequoias and Aspen trees are intertwined with each other. When strong winds blow the trees actually support and hold each other up. Isn't that a great metaphor for what we should be doing with every relationship we have?

Trees provide a great teaching about how our energy flows; and what we can do to create harmony. Our chakras represent an energy system that is three dimensional. Energy moves in all directions into and out from our body, with focal points at the chakras.

One interpretation of the Holy Cross is that it represents the energy within every human. The vertical axis is the energy that pours down from the heavens, through our body and into the earth. The horizontal axis is not only the energy that moves outwards from our chakras; it is also both a symbolic and literal interpretation of how we move through space. **Energetically you learn vertically; and you experience life horizontally**.

Place the intersection of this energetic cross at the point in the center of your brain about two inches behind the middle of your eyes. The location of your pineal gland, which is the shape of a pine cone (pineal) and the size of a pea. The third eye. The sixth chakra. You are a spirit that can move through space. It just happens that your spirit is temporarily enjoying the use of your physical body.

The vertical connection of energy between sky and earth is an important element of our stability, as it is for every tree. Instability can manifest in many ways that directly impact relationships. You can be spacey. Angry. Confrontational. Upset. Emotional. You are not yourself; and you don't know why. The biggest challenge we encounter is we don't recognize when we are not ourselves. We are in such a state of energetic disharmony that we do not know it. Other people see it; but we don't. It is a challenge to stop and say, "Hey, I am not myself. This isn't me." With presence and consciousness you can identify when you are out of sorts energetically.

EXERCISE

Ground Your Energy

One of the fastest ways to create stability is by grounding your energy. We have all heard the expression: "Are you grounded?" When you ground you are more in control of your reactions to events and other people. You need to ground your energy down into the earth, just as electricity does. There are several ways to do this. Let's consider the quickest first. Stop yourself from being engaged in the activity of the moment. Focus attention on feeling the energy in your body. If you don't feel anything, don't worry. Use your imagination. Imagination creates much more than fantasy. Imagination literally represents images in action (image-in-ation).

First, visualize tree-like trunks extending down from your physical feet into the ground below you. Let these trunks go down three feet. This provides a sense of physical stability. Second, as you breathe out visualize your energy going down through your body, through these roots, into the Earth. If you are sitting in a chair imagine that this energy is flowing down from your feet and the base of your spine. Do this for a minute, even when you are engaged in conversation, and see if you can feel the calming effect, the presence of the moment arise from grounding.

If you have a little more time you can conduct a longer and more sophisticated energy ceremony. Again, you can do this ceremony by yourself, with your eyes open or closed. You can also do it when you are with other people. From a sitting position visualize your body energy as a current, like electricity. Think of a bright orange/red color. The color of the robes of Tibetan monks. Visualize this energy field about three feet wide. Slightly wider than your own body. It encircles you.

Now, as you breathe out, visualize this circle of energy flowing downward through your body and feet into the ground. First, three feet, into the surface, the skin, of the Earth. Do this for twenty seconds. Now, let it move further down, twenty, thirty feet into the rocks, the bones of the Earth. Continue until you feel the effect of this grounding. Move the energy further down. A quarter mile. Just imagine it. Your energy reaches the gems, the organs of the Earth. Notice what you feel. Keep breathing and let your energy move down on every out breath. Finally, let it travel down several miles to touch the great crystals, the brains of the Earth. Hold this space for a minute, or two. When you are done, slowly open your eyes.

This ceremony is not about going down to reach the center of the Earth. It is about creating, opening, a channel of energy. The more grounded you are, the more you can recognize and explore time and space on your own terms. In other words, you won't be as easily pulled into the insanity or chaos that may be whirling around you. As with any type of exercise, the more you practice, the better and faster the results. Ideally you should be able to ground yourself in any situation in two minutes. That's a fast way to stabilize yourself and the situation!

Dissolve Energetic Cords that Tie You Down

Cowboys lasso calves. Fishermen snare fish. In both cases there is a period of time where the human is connected with a physical cord to an animal.

After the animal and human are finally brought together this rope or line is severed. What would happen if the cord didn't get cut? Could you imagine a cowboy who has thrown out and roped three, four, five calves all at the same time? Or, a deep sea fisherman who is simultaneously trying to pull in a half dozen swordfish? They'd be ripped into little pieces.

It is the same with our energy. When our energy gets dispersed in many directions we are energetically pulled apart. What we don't see, or recognize, is that we constantly create energetic cords between ourselves and many other people. Unlike the grounding energy cord that we make with the earth, these cords tug on us in different, not always positive, ways.

Probably the best example of a strong person-to-person energy cord that most people have experienced is when we are in love with someone (that includes parents and children). The connection is so strong that we often hear something like: "He or she really pulls on my heart strings." Everyone has heard of heart strings. It is a verbal expression of the energetic cord, the lasso, that exists between two people who care about each other.

A cord of love is a fantastic gift when both parties are actively engaged in the relationship. What about a connection that has an element of dependence? Or, the connection between yourself and someone who needs or wants to be in control of your life? Someone who would like to you continue to play a certain role that has been established by the story of the relationship? They are trying to sustain one or more of those unbroken habits and stories that you are now ready to move beyond. Dysfunctional relationships do not need to continue to have support on a physical or energetic level.

Even a "good" energy cord between friends may outlive it's usefulness. If the friendship ends, or ended years ago, one of you may still have an energetic connection to the other. You are not even aware of it, yet this friend continues to think about you once a month.

Imagine all the people you have known in your life. If they all had a physical rope wrapped around your waist you couldn't move. Sometimes energetic connections between people dissolve like feathery clouds that vanish as they are touched by the rays of the sun. Many times, however, you need to formally dissolve the energy cord. You need to disengage energetically because this unseen, unbroken connection remains intact and drains your energy.

There are obvious and not-so-obvious ways we can tell if these energy cords are still in place. Watch to see if a person in your life whom you have ended a relationship with continues to communicate with you; sends you holiday greetings; shows up in your life unexpectedly. It is obvious when Caller ID displays their phone number. It is not as evident when you have a dream about that person. You might not even remember the dream; and certainly not give it any credence in terms of direct communication. However, when people come to us in our dreams it usually signifies that they are either on our (subconscious) mind; or that they are thinking about us and would like to communicate. If it is someone you feel good about pick up your cell phone and give them a call. Odds are they'll say they were just thinking about you.

Regardless of the specific signals you receive, you may get signals that certain unwanted relationships may not be as severed as you thought. You are still attached; and an energetic connection may still be in place. It is very likely that one, or both of you, have not recognized or accepted on all levels that separation has occurred. Don't immediately jump to the conclusion that it is the "other person" who has not broken the connection. You might be holding on yourself.

There is another energy cord that commonly occurs. That is an energetic connection between you and the place you live. Especially true if you own your home and/or have put love into your physical environment, making it a special aspect of your life. You have fallen in love with where you live.

Certainly not a problem if you are living there. What if you are trying to sell your house? In that case your mind has committed to a separation. You want someone to buy your house. But there is a part of you that will miss the place. You grew up here. Your children grew up here. You fixed it just the way you want it. Whatever. What can happen when this strong energetic connection exists is that it becomes very difficult to leave; or the property does not sell very quickly. Just like the connection you have with people; you need to eliminate your energetic connection to the physical location to facilitate either your ability to move on, or the ability of the property to move on.

There exists the possibility to have both good and bad energetic connections. No need to get rid of anything good. You do, however, want to dissolve any connections that are not currently serving you or your higher self. Cutting and chopping may be effective; but isn't always the best way to go. If you envision a rope going directly into your pelvis you can understand that if you simply slice it a few inches in front of your body that the process is rather severe, and you still have a little rope stuck inside like a little sponge a surgeon accidently left during an operation. In fact, when you give or receive a knife as a gift there is an unspoken severing of the relationship. Notice if at any time in your life there was a gift of a knife and whether that relationship remains intact.

Here is a visualization technique that dissolves unwanted energetic connections. Your higher self has intelligence and abilities that go beyond what your mind can conceive. That is why it is called higher self. In my experience while the specifics of spiritual ceremony certainly play a role in the effectiveness of a transformational process; your own intention and focused attention are equally significant. That is because when you come from a place of sincerity and love, your higher self and the entire universe conspire to work on your behalf. This does not guarantee that you get what you want; only that movement will occur choreographed to create harmony.

In the case of energy cords let your mind quiet down for a minute. Ground yourself. Ask your higher self to recognize and identify any energetic cords that no longer serve you. If you specifically know of any such cords ask that they become apparent. Imagine your body filled with light. Now simply ask that all energy cords that do not serve you are returned to their owners. Send them love. Send them forgiveness. Be quiet and notice what you feel.

Forgiveness Opens Many Doors

The actions we perform in our life create the energy which connects us to other people. In many spiritual and religious traditions our actions not only define who we are; but also are the genesis of who we become in this life, and beyond. One of the most powerful actions we can engage in is that of forgiveness. It is also the very best way to actively engage in dissolving cords that bind us and hold us back.

On the Medicine Wheel, forgiveness appears on the South West of the compass. Forgiveness, like water, mirrors the movement of our emotions, and provides a quality that enables movement to occur in life. It offers an absence of constriction and contraction for your body and emotions. In the process of transformation, forgiveness provides a significant key.

Accept your own weaknesses, and those of other people. This will bring you closer to your prana body. When you totally accept what is present with non-judgmental awareness, it changes your future. You become comfortable and in harmony with yourself and others. Rejection, guilt, jealousy, hatred of your self and others all dissolve rapidly. You remain choice less with what is present. Every time your mind comes in with it's reaction, emotions and thoughts, go back to your prana body, your energy body, which lives in the present moment. This is where healing occurs. Acceptance in the present moment is critical for acceptance in the future.

Forgiveness goes hand-in-hand with compassion. In fact, forgiveness creates compassion for yourself. It is a win-win activity that brings harmony and success into life. Your mind may say, "I will never forgive so-and-so for this-and-that." It appears to both your mind and ego that a lack of forgiveness, possibly even outright revenge, will ultimately create harmony. If the other person finally receives the same treatment that you got, or some form of punishment, then everything is even and you can move on.

Unfortunately energy does not work that way. Instead of creating a net-zero effect you actually add to the original offense. This is why rivalries and wars spiral upward. Even if someone "wins" it only creates a temporary holding pattern until the other party has an opportunity to get even.

Global Harmony Begins With You

To change the exterior world, the world that surrounds you, you need only change yourself. Transformation of your inner condition automatically adjusts and changes your exterior life. Your thoughts, emotions and the energy of your chakras are all inner conditions. Forgiveness is also inward. Look towards an aspect of yourself that is mirrored in the events, situations and actions of others around you.

You can forgive at any time to receive the benefits. It is actually better, although perhaps not easier, to forgive immediately because you don't suffer the consequences from anger and frustration that build and store themselves in your body and mind. Mehmet Ali Agca fired shots at Pope

John Paul II in St Peter's Square on 13 May 1981, hitting him four times. Agca served nearly 20 years in Italian jails for the attempted murder. The pontiff later visited him in jail. What is amazing is that John Paul said he forgave Agca within seconds of being shot.

Forgive yourself. It is not uncommon that when you perceive forgiveness you first go to the other person. In other words you come up with a list of people, groups and events that need your forgiveness. That's fine. But the nature of this suggests that you also have to forgive yourself for something in the relationship. This is because *you* are the person who is thinking about, and suffering from, the story.

Let's be clear about forgiveness. It is not: "I accept that you recognize the errors of your ways, and the mistake that you made. I totally forgive you." That is DEFINITELY NOT forgiveness. That continues to hold your power over the other person. That is your ego trying to protect and enhance your personal power in an artificial pretense of forgiveness. Remember, forgiveness is more about you than it is about the other person.

Forgive yourself for holding onto the anger that is hurting you, not them. It is the ultimate in personal responsibility and transformation to realize that forgiveness of external relationships and events is designed to help us forgive our own internal conflicts. This is true forgiveness. And, it feels great.

Global Peace Happens Now

Forgiveness and compassion. The Dalai Lama's recipe for global peace is so simple we can not believe it. Our mental conditioning creates a story that makes this an enormous undertaking. Surely it will take years, maybe centuries, before the human race learns all these lessons. Don't contract to that. When we experience one day, one rotation of planet earth, where enough people on the globe engage in pure compassion, love and forgiveness, the world we live in will shift.

At the public opening of The Great Stupa of Dharmakaya, Shambhala's Sakyong Mipham Rinpoche said, "Compassion is a viable means of engaging in the world's issues. Compassion and the path of peace are the best, most practical way of sustaining the world in the mental happiness and physical preservation of the earth. In the long term aggression does not work." Making the point that it does not take a large number of people to make a significant change he said, "In a very short amount of time Tibetans, and the Dalai Lama, have become globally known for our single minded focus on Compassion. We are statistically a small percentage of the global population."

It only requires the focused attention of a portion of the population to rapidly create a global shift. Mahatma Gandhi's famous quote: "Be the change you want to see in the world." You are this change. When you give love from your Heart Center your friends, loved ones, colleagues and the entire planet change. Instantly.

Notes and Experiences

CONSCIOUSNESS: 5
CONNECT TO SOURCE

Sage, my Australian Shepherd, is fourteen. That is old for any dog, but especially an Aussie. The most noticeable sign of her aging is the soft grey hairs that surround her muzzle, and significant loss of hearing. If I shout her name like a war cry she turns and looks at me like she's just heard a faint whisper. Even with the early stage of hip dysplasia she enjoys walks. I didn't think anything unusual would happen as we start an outing. But within minutes a fox decides to visit and share another lesson. I see the fox out of the corner of my eye. It is crouching beside a large pine tree waiting for a squirrel to move past. Sage visions her own prey. Before I can turn to grab her collar she flies toward the fox. All I see is fur streaking into the forest.

Two years ago I would not have given the situation a second thought. But, with the hearing loss, I know there is a serious problem. I feel my own fear in my solar plexus. A deep, shouting pain. This is not the suburbs. It's thousands of acres with a few houses sprinkled in. If Sage follows the fox long enough she'll be tired and disoriented with no ability to hear my call. I run after her, screaming. It's already too late. There is no sign of my dog or the fox. I continue the search. First along the path they took. Then, retracing my steps, back and in another direction. My mind fills with stories. Why didn't I grab her faster? Sage will get lost and die in the woods. Sage will be found by some other hiker who will call the number on her dog tag. Sage will lose her dog tag in the chase. I search for hours. Yelling. Sobbing.

Finally, I sit down on a log. I am not tired; but I *have* run out of ideas. There is nothing more I can do that will change the outcome. I decide to pray. I ask the supreme god, the universe, every teacher I've had and every angel that I do and don't recognize to lend a hand. And, I stop thinking. I have done what I can and the outcome is out of my hands. I close my eyes. If you had a stopwatch you would not believe it. In less than a minute I feel a cold, wet nose touch my arm. My dog has found me.

The Human World Manifests Reality

The animal, plant and mineral worlds use prana, energy, in a pre-pro-grammed manner. They do not make conscious choices; but rather use prana primarily for the preservation of their existence. Unlike the human world, the other worlds are not burdened with self image. They never use energy to consider how they look, or feel. Their use of energy is sponta-neous. Their only concern is their immediate survival and the survival of their species.

Humans have an animal body; but our powerful minds enable us to have self conscious awareness. For example, we can and often do spend a great deal of time wondering what other people think about us. A better meaning for self conscious involves being aware of rather than afraid of your actions. We also spend hours delving into stories that occur in the past and the future. This use of our energy to focus attention on events that are out of the current moment gives us the ability to dream and create in a way that other species can not. We can envision the creation of a great cathedral, or a space ship that travels to Saturn. The vision of the future becomes manifest reality as we focus our energy and the energy of others on our dreams. This is significant!

The innate powers or abilities of the human species encompass the use of energy, consciousness, time, space, inspiration and imagination. These divine powers come free of charge. You don't have to buy a ticket or pay an hourly fee to have complete access to the most exceptional abilities.

It is not uncommon for spiritual seekers to pursue new abilities. There are endless stories of great masters who can manifest objects, heal people, see events in the future and be in several locations at the same time. In yoga these powers are called siddhis.

We already have divine powers we don't use, or use improperly. Indeed our abilities are so powerful that we can easily, and unconsciously, work against the natural harmony that nature strives toward. We can, for example, work a ten hour day without taking a break even though our body tells us we need to stop and take a walk. We can use our self image to create stories that artificially color daily experience. "I am not good enough, smart enough, fast enough"; or "I *am* better, smarter, faster."

Energy, nature, our higher selves and god are constantly speaking to us. Their language is silent and we haven't been trained to hear this non-verbal communication. If we learn how to converse, and how to listen, we can easily understand and penetrate the truth of what needs to be done to create balance and joy in our life and on the planet.

Talking and Listening to the Universe

A foundation of all faith, prayer is how we speak to the universe, and to god. It doesn't matter if you are kneeling in a church, swimming in the ocean or sitting in a bowling alley. Prayer as a form of communication is available 24/7. Prayer opens your true nature and lets you to access issues that concern you deeply. It allows you to formalize essential communication. Prayer is extremely personal whether it is used as gratitude or to send out an S.O.S.

Know that you do not pray to change God's mind. Envision God as an incarnate being sitting comfortably before you on a leather Ottomon. You finish your prayer. He rubs his chin in thoughtful repose before saying, "You know I never saw it that way before. You are absolutely right. If you really need that in your life count me in." Prayer is a technique that helps you energetically become more receptive to a plan that is already developed at a higher level.

You are *both* the prayer and the receiver of the prayer. Prayers are foremost from you to yourself. Otherwise you are saying that God is outside of you. The Sanskrit phrase is *Tat Tvam Asi*. Translated, this means: "Thou art That." When you offer prayers to God, the first recipient must be yourself. But not your ego. You pray and then immediately release it. Let go of any holding onto a desire for or against a specific outcome. Now your prayer can enter a unified energy field where it can be heard by the cosmic consciousness and acted upon. You step out of your mind and accept, "Not my will, but Thine, be done."

That is what happened when I gave up looking for my dog. I got out of my own way and allowed the energetic intention to move beyond the confines of my own mind. Universal prana is an infinite energy and information field. I do not need to understand the mechanics of how the universe, or God, receives and responds to my prayer; nor how my dog receives her instinctive energetic signals. What occurs is beyond words or definition. As Swami Kripalu states: "Mind is finite and limited, while God is infinite and limitless. How can speech have access to those places where the mind has none? Speech can describe sensory experiences but not extra-sensory ones."

Prayers are always heard. The challenge lies in hearing the response. Meditation is one way you can listen to God's replies. Another is to watch carefully and see what manifests in your life. Know that answers to your prayers may not be exactly what you desire. Certainly not what your ego craves. Stay open to the possibility that the manifestation of a positive response may show up in a way that is not what you had *in your mind*. Because the opposite of what you want may be exactly what you need.

I Meet My Guru

I breathe deeper and faster. I release just as quickly. My arms raise with every breath in; fall with every breath out. "So-Hum. So-Hum. So-Hum." The Mantra screams out from a red, battery-operated megaphone. My movement and breathing moves in the same rhythm. My eyes are closed and I am barely aware that I am sitting in a room with thirty other people. I can not remember my name and the fact that So-Hum means "I am That" has completely disappeared from my consciousness.

Every weekend for six months I drive a hundred and twenty miles to a small, secluded yoga studio that has a stellar view of magnificent Pikes Peak. It was on the pinnacle of this mountain where, in 1893, English professor Katherine Lee Bates teaching a summer class at Colorado College was inspired to pen the poem *America The Beautiful*.

If I open my eyes I can see the peak clearly. But I am doing Yoga Kriya. A process that effectively and rapidly disengages the mind and the ego from any control they have over the body or soul. The studio, open to the public, belongs to and sits on the private property of John McAfee, who is now vehemently shouting, "What you put into this is what you'll get out. So-Hum. So-Hum." John is widely known as the founder of McAfee antivirus software. He also has a passion for yoga.

The Kriya takes several hours. I feel light. In fact I feel like my body is a hollow, little shell and I am somewhere else. We open our eyes. In the corner of the studio there is a gentleman dressed head to toe in yogic apparel. He has a face that is both gentle and beautiful. John makes a quick introduction to his guest who has been observing the Kriya. His name is Yogi Amrit Desai. We all begin to slowly stand up. Yogi Desai walks toward me with no apparent intention of stopping. But, as he passes, he leans over and whispers casually, "I saw great manifestations."

I have no idea what he's talking about. I am still tripped out from having left my body. We enter John's house for refreshments. Within minutes I have made my way with a plate of fruit over to sit on a very large white sofa beside this yoga master and his friend and companion Modini. I have found my guru. Or, my Guru has found me.

Are You Out of Your Mind?

Again and again spiritual texts and teachers tell us the same thing. Live in the present moment. Be Here Now. The future hasn't happened and the past is a memory. The message is clear. Like a mantra. Why then is it such a challenge to live this?

Because of the incredible power of the human mind. The mind is the medium through which we create our ego. The mind creates and then lives in a maze of habitual patterns. The mind also envisions dreams of future oriented goals which often become the primary focus of our precious energy.

Yogi Amrit Desai is better known by his nickname Gurudev, great teacher. Gurudev began bringing the sacred yoga teachings of his own master Swami Kripalvanandji to the United States in the 1960's. The yoga society Gurudev founded in Pennsylvania eventually grew to become Kripalu Center for Yoga and Health, one of the largest centers of its kind. Gurudev demystifies the process by which we can move beyond the normal use of our mind to access our inherent connection to spirit and live effortlessly in the present.

Seven years after I first met Gurudev, I find myself sitting beside this great yoga master as I drive him to a meeting near the Amrit Yoga Institute in Salt Springs, Florida. Thirty minutes go by. We say little but enjoy the drive through the Ocala National Forest. I am a little concerned that we may have taken a wrong turn and may arrive late. Gurudev turns to me, smiles and says, "Bill, it is amazing how quiet my mind is."

I take his sharing as a profound revelation and also a teaching. I could sense the meaning of his words. Intellectually I understand that the entire purpose of all aspects of all forms of yoga is to quiet the fluctuations of the mind. Noticing that my own internal dialog is increasing I ask, "Gurudev it is not always easy for me to have a quiet mind. Why is that?"

"It's common. Shakti, energy, manifests in your body in the present moment. So your prana body lives in the present," he explains. "But, your mental and emotional bodies live in the past and future. When you have a reaction it is a reaction not to the event, or the person, but to the original cause of that reaction. It could have been an event long ago. Do not identify yourself with your reaction. That is only a process. Release immediately. Become a witness and come back to the present moment again and again."

As Gurudev speaks I notice that I am becoming less concerned about the consequence of our route. I find myself calmly accepting the unknown outcome of our route.

Gurudev continues, "We create problems when our prana, our energy, is engaged by our ego mind to get more, or less, of something. We use our energy inappropriately. All problems can be solved in the present moment. But they cannot be solved in the past or the future. It is impossible to change your entire life. You can only change one moment. But that is enough."

I want to simultaneously understand this teaching and use the knowledge. I summarize my understanding with a statement and a question, "So, when our mind chooses that it likes or dislikes something it interrupts the experience we are having at the moment. How do we tell our mind to shut up?"

"Use you breath to interrupt the mind in it's process of choice. You can also use the ajna chakra, the third eye, to cripple the thoughts and be present. You do this so the mind does not disrupt the dance between energy and consciousness."

Just as my mind formulates an entire series of questions about the dance of energy and consciousness we arrive at our destination. The present moment once again makes itself known.

Early the next morning, sitting comfortably in lotus, Gurudev gives Darshan to a small group. He beams as he continues with the topic we were on. "Everything in the universe consists of two primary properties. Consciousness and energy. Shiva and shakti. When consciousness combines with energy it manifests as all that we see, touch, feel and experience. The formless is the background for the form. Just like the planets and the stars sit out in space and space itself is the background. All forms are a manifestation of shakti, energy."

As Gurudev speaks, I realize that all the four worlds, mineral, plant, animal and human contain consciousness and energy. The only difference is the level or the manner in which they display the combination. Science certainly agrees on the similarity of all objects at the atomic level of protons, electrons and neutrons. With their scanning tunneling microscopes (STM) scientists can see the energy; but not the consciousness. And consciousness is where we want to play. It is where we can commune with rocks, plants, animals and each other.

"Energy can take any form it wants," Gurudev continues. "Energy is always looking for a vessel to hold it. Everything can be a vehicle for prana. Even the human body is a vessel. Each of us is Shiva (consciousness) and Shakti (energy) and we use them to imagine and create our life. At the same time we are all timeless spirits coming through time bound bodies. This is an inborn enigma."

Gurudev takes a sip of water, almost as an intentional pause to allow meaning to sink in with his devoted audience. "Consciousness and energy are one. They separate only for the sake of diversity, but they are happy as one. When God splits into two, he also becomes Shiva and Shakti. When ego splits into two it becomes happiness and unhappiness. Then, since ego usually selects happiness over unhappiness, it automatically sets the stage to receive unhappiness because it is impossible not to get the opposite," he pauses. "Does anyone have a question or want to share?"

A young woman clears her throat and asks, "Gurudev, sometimes I have negative thoughts. And I get mad at myself because I think that I am creating my own unhappiness with these thoughts. How can I stop them?"

Gurudev turns slightly and reaches to pick a flower out of a vase. He admires it for a moment before speaking, "Look, I have a flower." He places it back in the vase. "Look I can put it away. I am not the flower just like you are not your negative thoughts. If someone else has negative thoughts do you have a problem? No. Never. Thought forms have a beginning and an end. They are a subtle form of creation. Your power is to let your mind have negative thoughts and not choose for or against them. Then, they naturally vanish."

As Gurudev pauses, my thoughts bring me back to a training session with A.G. Mohan. A.G. Mohan was a personal student of

Sri T. Krishnamacharya for 18 years. Krishnamacharya had other students including BKS Iyengar, K. Pattabhi Jois and Indra Devi. Sri Mohan describes how yoga therapy can be used to release the programmed mind from it's jail cell to eliminate habitual patterns, negative thoughts and depression. He explains, "There is only the now (vrtti) and the memory or latent impressions (samskaras). Our thoughts and feelings are the activities of the mind that come from latent impressions. This is a cycle that continues again and again. We create so many cycles that we don't act consciously most of the time, but rather from habitual patterns. We must break our cycles to make a change.

For example, with depression try interrupting the thought process by using sound. Chant the mantra *OM* or *OM Namaha* (this thought does not belong to me). Practice it twice a day for fifteen minutes. Say, "There is nothing wrong with me. My mind is momentarily confused. Use free will to become free of your samskaras. The danger is that you create a new thought cycle. Whatever happens you get the opposite as well. Happiness comes with sadness. So you use Om Namaha when you are happy and when you are sad. Because neither belong to you. You are not happiness or sadness."

I go to lunch with A.G. Mohan, his wife Indra and son Ganesh. The Mohan's have made yoga a family affair. I love them not only because of this; but also because they have created an absolute treasure chest of extremely practical and effective applications where yoga is used as a therapeutic process for a variety of illnesses. Yoga therapy. Mohan elaborates on the philosophical foundation that underlies our ability to move past behavioral patterns. He says, "When we realize that all we see is only light. Then, when something changes in our perception, perhaps we see something new, we can not like or dislike it because it is only more light. We begin to be enlightened."

A.G. and Ganesh show me some specific breathing techniques and postures that can help with both my posture and my asthma. Five years later I meet them again at a yoga conference where we are both teaching workshops. A.G. Mohan sits beside me at one of those large round tables. He doesn't appear to know me. I am just about to re-introduce myself when he smiles and says, "Bill, you look so different. I didn't recognize you at first because you look physically different. Taller." Ironically it is the simple exercise that he himself taught me that helped with the transformation.

Non-Doing Awareness

A.G. Mohan acknowledges that neither good thoughts nor bad thoughts belong to us. For people that are having serious problems with their thoughts, he suggests a therapeutic approach to working with thought patterns. I envision a chalkboard where you erase what is on it so you can have a blank slate to put on new writing.

Gurudev advocates a slightly different approach. One that on the surface sounds simple. Non-doing, non-reactive, choice-less awareness. He says, "Live your life at ease. Go to a space of non-doing. God realization is non-doing. When the doer disappears you end duality and create polarity. Thoughts themselves are not the problem. They just keep coming and going. It is attachment to them that creates a time-space event where you become a doer. Then your ego wants to create a result that is dependent upon space and time."

Always trying to get to the practical application I ask, "Gurudev, how do we consciously become non-doers?"

"Energy relates to energy but not through the medium of the mind," he replies. "In other words your thoughts obscure the energetic meaning that is the real truth. When you remove your mind from superimposing on your prana body you achieve polarity. When you go there consciously, you superimpose intention onto your prana body for complete integration. Everything you are doing gets done better when you are integrated. Deliberate action with integration nurtures your being."

"All thoughts to achieve something, or do something, create conflict. When your prana is enslaved by your fragmented mind it is reduced. You are tired and stressed. You don't need to *arrive* to be successful. You will never get there. Your ego cannot do it for you. You must go to a timeless dimension where you don't cause or determine the effect. Doing is not a solution. Transform your unconscious energies to understand that there can be action in *non-doing*. This is hard to understand as we have been trained our entire life that action translates as doing something. We are normally like a one winged bird. We are flapping one wing extremely hard. It is time to use our other wing. The wing of non-doing. Tune into your innate abilities without setting up goals."

The Left Brain, Right Brain and Non-Doing

Our brains come ready made in two distinct hemispheres.   Unlike two halves of a sliced grapefruit, the two sides of our brain actually view the world in different ways. An understanding of this unusual co-creation of our world view came to light about fifty years ago when, in the 1960's, American psychobiologist and Nobel Prize winner Roger W. Sperry discovered that each hemisphere of the human brain has a distinct way of thinking. And, that every person generally favors one hemisphere over the other. Here are the main distinctions:

Right Brain

> ➤ This hemisphere is visual and processes information intuitively.
> ➤ It first "looks" at the whole and then at the details.
> ➤ On a physical level the right hemisphere controls the left side of our body.

Left Brain

> ➤ This hemisphere is verbal and processes information in an analytical and sequential fashion.
> ➤ It first looks at pieces, then puts together the whole.
> ➤ On a physical level the left hemisphere controls the right side of our body.

LEFT	RIGHT
Verbal and word based	Visual thinker
Analytical and logical	Intuitive
Work step-by-step	See whole, then details
Highly organized	Not overly organized
Good sense of time	No sense of time
Spelling and math are easy	Trouble with spelling and mathematics
Usually read manuals	Don't read manuals
Rarely use gestures	Talk with your hands

At a glance you can see that, depending upon the circumstances, we need both sides of our brains to function. Many simple projects, say painting your bedroom, require both sides of the brain. When you start many projects you need to be able to "visualize" the outcome in your mind (RIGHT). How will periwinkle blue look and should the ceiling be white? Then, you need to pull a number of things together simultaneously (RIGHT). Buy the paint, brushes, drop clothes, move the furniture, tape the windows. And finally, look critically at what you're doing (LEFT). Is this actually working?

The Right Brain is clearly comfortable with non-doing. It is intuitive. It has no sense of time. It can't read product manuals. It lives in the here and now. To achieve a shift in consciousness; to flap our other wing; requires that we access, empower and use our right brain.

Gurudev explains how this important gateway works. He says, "Your right brain helps you re-align with that part of your being that exists beyond the confines of your intellect. This shift in perspective allows you to permanently resolve perceived problems, and habitual patterns at their root. You can release habitual patterns that bind you and cause to create the same situations over and over. You can access the infinite field of energy and information in which collective knowledge, creative solutions and skillful action arise. You learn to draw happiness from the present moment rather than uncertain promises of the future. And, you stop reacting to life and start living in harmony with it."

From Drawing Trees to Living in the Moment

Don Moulton taught me how to draw a tree. I was thirteen. My father Gerald was chairman of the art department at Bucknell University. Don taught painting and drawing. Over a course of months Don showed me how to see the world and transfer what I saw onto paper. Trees were my favorite subject. I would start with the trunk; then carefully add branches and leaves.

Ten years later as a documentary filmmaker I chose Don as the subject for my celluloid canvas. Don was a prominent artist. He had found his muse. Apples and rocks. He would search the world for gorgeous apples and lingams, beautiful meditative rocks. Then he would shape and meticulously paint three dimensional versions. They were easily five, six feet wide. They would hang on a wall as if they had grown there. The owners of the majestic John Hancock Building, a two-million-square-foot tower in downtown Boston, commissioned Don's apples.

When I walk in, Don's classroom invokes a comfortable feeling of the textures and aromas that compose artistic expression. The smell of oil paint and turpentine fills the room. Twenty wooden easels, each with canvas and artist, are scattered around the room. All attention focuses on the male model in the center of the room. Don, sporting gold rimmed glasses, a yacht cap and a blue sweater, looks more like a sailor than an art teacher. He shuffles around the periphery moving up to student painters who appear to be in need of direction. He watches a young woman who is holding her paintbrush with indecision. He offers, "Think space, and it will look like space. Try not to get involved with that jacket too much. Just deal with it as one color."

He moves to a young man who, surprisingly, is wearing a completely white shirt that does not have a spot of paint on it. The fellow stares at his painting. It has a complete face that closely resembles the face of the model, but there are large white spaces where there should be shoulders and a torso.

Don places his hand on the artists shoulder. Like a consoling pastor, he suggests, "My son, you should bring up that color. If lightning were to strike our model and he was carried off to heaven, you could stop. Your painting would be complete. At any point it is complete." Like a spiritual guide with a sense of humor, Don's insights give his students knowledge that art has a philosophical aspect. The satisfaction that is available every moment is more significant than the final outcome. The young man nods slowly as if this powerful concept has merit. He repeats softly, "At any point it is complete."

EXERCISE

The Random Line Technique

Why is it so important to connect to source or learn how to feel our own energy and consciously respond to its direction? Why should we ever let the right brain sit in the driver's seat? Simple. Because our own intuitive knowing, which comes directly from listening carefully to the signals of our energy body, can guide us in all areas of life. Results are far superior to what the mathematically oriented left brain can accomplish. This is where animals have it hands down over humans. They simply respond to instincts driven by prana. We get in our own way with thoughts that actually slow us down. You want to make the right decisions in your life faster. You want to become healthy. Listen to prana.

If the right brain is a doorway for us to walk through and connect with source, shiva and shakti, non-linear, non-logical, astral worlds then how do we open the door? Every muscle in the body, and every ability of the conscious and unconscious mind becomes stronger with usage. Look at the practice it requires to learn how to play the guitar, dance, cook, run a marathon. Anything. It's just that most of the time we engage in activities where the left mind still dominates.

Notice that your Right Brain is a visual thinker. It works better with images than with words. Visuals are energetically at a higher level than words. The random line technique is a simple art exercise that Pablo Picasso, among others, have used. Not surprisingly, Picasso defines God as an artist. He says, "God is really only another artist. He invented the giraffe, the elephant and the cat. He has no real style. He just goes on trying other things."

Grab a pen, pencil and piece of paper. Drop your pen anywhere on the paper. Now start drawing a squiggle line. Any line. Move the pen randomly around. Line over line. It does not matter. The main thing here is that you DO NOT consciously guide your hand. This is not about thinking. It is about going with the flow of your own energy or prana. After you see that your graphic wanderings have created some patterns you can reconnect your line to the place you started. That's it. If you are still feeling artistic you can start to fill in the spaces with different colors like paint by numbers. Who knows? The point of the exercise is to begin to connect at a non mental level with your energy body.

The Dance of Prana

Humans dance. Our original relationship to dance was to worship, heal and celebrate. Native cultures correctly view nature as an expression of God. It is appropriate to imitate nature through physical movement and sound. The origins of dance are a method of learning from and honoring nature by connecting to spirit.

Mimic the motions of an elk and learn how it moves with strength and agility in the darkest night. Swim with a dophin and experience weightless movement through space. Follow the stalking movements of your cat and discover what it is like to focus your mental attention with the use of your body. Recall your animal totem. Does it have physical abilities or characteristics that you can emulate?

Because animals respond instantly to prana we can learn about this connection by imitating their natural rhythms and dances. For centuries Shaolin Kung Fu styles developed around animal totems. Shaolin Kung Fu training was as much a method of health and fitness as it was fighting and self defense. Over time Shaolin Kung Fu created the Five Animal styles which use animals and their innate characteristics for training. They include tiger, panther, crane, snake and dragon. For example, snake trains chi or internal energy. Snake is about precision, speed and secret knowledge. Snake movements flow and weave like a snake and emphasize use of fingers. The Snake focuses on vital points with eyes and the throat being common targets.

Dance is integral to all religions and spiritual practices. Consider the Whirling Dervish, a member of the Sufi Muslim sect known as Tariqah. Dervishes are Sufis who create and share wisdom, medicine, poetry and enlightenment. The famous Persian poet Rumi whose immense works of poetry are still being translated was a Dervish. The whirling dance is the practice of the Mevlevi Order in Turkey.

A Dervish whirls in a precise rhythm. Through spinning they represent the Earth as it revolves on its axis while orbiting the Sun. By whirling the Dervish empties all thoughts. They move into a trancelike, ecstatic state where, released from the body, they even conquer dizziness. Dance, spinning and emulating the movements of nature are one way to get in touch with and experience the natural movement of prana. Any form of dance brings this connection.

Swami Kripalu and Gurudev became adapt at the free flow of prana. Kripalu relished spontaneous, free flowing dance and mudras, or hand movements. Gurudev occasionally performs spontaneous asana flows that are quite amazing. In this state of free flow, the physical body can move in ways that it cannot conceive of during normal consciousness. Swami Kripalu describes it this way: "When the best dancer is dancing, a whole crowd can find themselves drawn into concentration. .... I dance and sing constantly in my meditation room. This isn't simply art, but a form of meditation." Prana creates the dance. Dance is an expression of prana. You are the dance.

Let Go of All Doing

I see a small one inch ad in a local newspaper that announces Swamiji, the incarnation of Shri Shivabalayogi, will give a presentation at a local church. My mind creates a story about what it will be like when I meet this renowned guru. I am quickly corrected as the room is smaller than I imagine. There are perhaps twenty people in attendance. For a minute I wonder if the snow has kept Swamiji from coming. He arrives. Wearing white robes he moves to the front of the room to sit in a white chair. He has a translator because his command of English is limited. Instead of a spiritual discourse he beings with a one hour silent meditation. I discover later that this is his style. Silent teachings create inner transformation.

For a guru an hour of meditation is an appetizer. For most people it is a slow motion, five course meal. I sit in the front row, cross legged because this is more comfortable. My eyes are closed. I finally get over how long this is going to be, and that I did not get a lecture. I start to calm down. Suddenly I relax much more deeply. Like a switch has been turned.

Then I sit, without thoughts, until the lights come on. I find that I don't want to open my eyes. After singing Bhajans, simple spiritual songs, I move up to thank Swamiji and ask a question. His face beams with contentment and happiness. He asks my name.

I tell him my Sanskrit name, given to me by Gurudev. "Pradip," I say, pronouncing it "Prah-deep."

He smiles and says, "That is a good name."

Through his translator I ask whether during meditation it is advisable to try and watch the energy. After hearing the question he looks directly at me and in slow English says, "No. Do nothing. The energy and your body will automatically do what they need to do."

The external circumstances of the world create a variety of left brained pressures. You know the list. Make so much money to pay the bills. Advance your career. Have a certain physical appearance. Make sure your relationships are as good as those in the movies. Because of worldly pressures we use the mind to solve perceived problems. We believe that the left brain, so good at analysis, can pick the right career, stocks, clothing and real estate. The result is that our prana suffers.

Prana is your connection to universal spirit. But your mind, especially your left brain and ego, want control of even this. What you want to practice is how to yield to the movement and functions of prana. The best way to hear and feel your prana is by not listening to your mind. There is the catch. In order to understand prana you need to understand your mind. You need the blessings of your mind to be able to choose and accept the path of prana.

The practice required is not one of mental cogitation. You can not force your left brain to turn itself off. Nor can you put your ego into a "time out" box. You can ask own mind for permission to enter a new space. Literally. Ask your own ego and your mind for their permission to enter the deepest level of non-doing, detached, choiceless awareness.

Your mind is the gateway to other states of consciousness. You need to recognize your mind for what it is. An instrument of your soul. Just as your eyes are an instrument for vision and your ears and instrument for hearing. The mind is a complicated instrument that needs to work for you. Like a fancy screwdriver. You don't let a screwdriver take over the construction of your new deck. You use it to plow in screws and then put it back in the tool belt.

Sakyong, Jamgon Mipham Rinpoche provides a great analogy. He compares the way most people use their mind to the way a dog responds when you throw a stick. The mind instinctively chases each and every thought. Keep throwing sticks and a dog will chase until it wears itself out. Keep thinking thoughts and your mind will run after every one. You want to train your mind to be more like a lion. Throw a stick for a lion. The lion does not look at and run for the stick. Instead the lion looks directly at the person who throws the stick. Calm your mind by seeing where the thoughts are coming from. Who is throwing them, and for what purpose?

Gurudev has perfected a form of yoga that naturally enhances the ability of the right brain and opens practitioners to prana. The Amrit Method™ involves two opposite, yet complimentary processes. First, you perform a deliberate action (use the left brain). Then you relax and let go (use the right brain). The result is that you don't have to work to achieve a meditative state of consciousness. It happens automatically. Gurudev describes it this way, "You step out of the mind and into the spirit that you are. You witness transitory events without reaction to them. You connect to source."

Cosmic Consciousness versus Collective Consciousness

Step back 15 billion years. That incomprehensible amount of time is when scientists believe the Big Bang occurred. At that moment all of the matter and energy of space was contained at one point. The Big Bang was not a conventional explosion. It was not Diet Coke and Mentos. Rather, it was an event that began to fill all space with the particles of the embryonic universe. Energy and consciousness rushing outwards infinity.

Some of this elixir creates the countless variety of physical objects. Yet there is one other aspect to the mixture. It is the energetic consciousness that permeates the space between physical objects and is contained inside objects themselves. This is cosmic consciousness. It is the field that allows shamans to travel through time and space for healing. It is the medium through which intuition, foresight and non-spoken communication travel faster than the speed of light. It is contained within you. And, when you passionately argue or make love to someone, you are nothing more or less incredible than one facet of the Big Bang interacting with another facet.

Do not confuse cosmic consciousness with collective consciousness. It is apples and oranges. Collective consciousness is the very temporary set of beliefs that a large group of people have. It is neither true, nor permanent. It is the collective fear or enthusiasm about the economy. It is the collective prejudice for or against a certain group of people. Because it represents the energy and consciousness of a large number of people, the collective consciousness has considerable power and sway over our thoughts and emotions. However, at it's core, it is totally artificial.

Cosmic consciousness, on the other hand, is much larger and time transcendent. The etymology of the word *cosmic* derives from the Greek word *kosmos* which means order. There is also an inherent vastness to the cosmic that exceeds what any group of people, even the population of the entire planet, can conceive at any time.

Surrender to Consciousness

Surrender is a word that sometimes invokes a negative reaction. For thousands of years citizens of the world have created a global culture that prides itself on crafting and being in control of it's destiny. We do not like to lose - a game, a business deal, a relationship or a war. Like prayer, surrender has the potential to connect you to source. In fact there are many ways we can benefit, and win, through surrender.

Many forms of spiritual practice focus on learning to let go of our ego. We surrender our ego. This form of surrender relates to all of the things we want to accomplish or win in life. Our mind and ego tell us that we want to accomplish or create a defined outcome. Naturally, when we don't see that outcome occur we get upset because we feel like we are not winning, not creating our destiny. Instead, if we surrender to what is happening we can accept what is happening right now.

There is a common resting pose done in every yoga class in the world. It is Balasana, Child's Pose. You sit on the floor, squat towards your heals, bend forward to rest your forehead on the ground and lay your hands down beside your head. This resting pose is actually a pose of surrender. You are prostrate. Your head is bowed. You are in supplication with your heart raised above your head. It is a defenseless position where you accept what is, as it is. Someone could come up and kick you. The act provides an opening where you accept wisdom, grace and actions that are beyond your own personal will.

Balasana is strikingly similar to the Sajdah posture, done five times a day during Salat, the Islamic ritual prayer. During this position Muslims recite: "Subhaana rabbiyal. Alaa, Allahu Akbar." Translated: *Glory to my Lord, the Most High. God is great.* Abu Huraira, a companion of the Islamic prophet Muhammad, and the narrator of the Hadith reported that the messenger of Allah said: "The nearest a servant comes to his Lord is when he is prostrating himself…"

One translation of the Sanskrit mantra "Om Namah Shivaya" is this: *I surrender to consciousness.* What does this mean? When you surrender to consciousness, which is considerably different than willpower, you allow yourself the opportunity to let the wisdom and order of the cosmic determine an outcome. You can rest comfortably knowing that cosmic consciousness contains wisdom and foresight that no group of people can construct within a purely mental framework.

When you allow yourself to surrender to consciousness and to what is present; the opening and understanding that you receive enables you to accept the current situation and future outcomes. This creates new windows and opportunities by which you accomplish goals and outcomes that you are unable to manifest willfully. By surrendering, you win.

Drop into Silence and Experience Consciousness

Surrender is an experience, not a definition. An experience that requires you do nothing, which can be difficult. When you surrender YOU are silent and still. Even stillness is a form of expression of prana. When you drop into this space you feel presence. A non-involved, non-judgemental presence. It is a space of meditative awareness.

Getting here can be a challenge. Not only because it is uncommon, but perhaps because you don't know why you should do it. Marketing theory suggests we need to understand the benefits of a product before we really want to own it. Imagine you have a super hero ability to shape shift into any form. Not just physical objects, but also sounds, light, energy. You disappear, become the form, then return to yourself. How cool would that be?

The perceiver (that is you) merges with the object (that is everything else) and you are completely at peace with what is. No matter what is. The perceiver and the object of perception merge. Why merge? Because normally you only experience the values that you place, implant, on the objects of your perception.

Think about an apple. It sits in front of you. Depending upon your past experience with apples this particular piece of fruit might look like a beautiful piece of healthy fruit. If you had a Snow White experience perhaps it would appear to be a deadly, poisonous object. It could be a home for worms.... a decoration... the precursor to apple pie, an object for a still life painting. You make of it what you will. The apple is just sitting there being an apple. Furthermore, the perceiver (still you) is reflected in the act of perception. If you are suspicious that every apple might be poisonous what does that say about your world?

The same thing applies with people. But it is more complicated because we see people over time. Apples don't have that kind of shelf life. Each time we see someone we carry our previous experience and perception into the current moment. We are not really seeing them. We are seeing who we thought they used to be. That is one reason that meeting new people can be so refreshing.

Wouldn't it be nice to see things as they really are? No more. No less. To merge with the perceived. You can. Silence and stillness are keys. When you are very silent and still you can disappear. The knower merges with the known. Then unity happens. In this state of complete relaxation there is absence of judgment. Absence of judgment represents absence of you as the doer.

The Connection of Breath and Consciousness

How do you consciously achieve unity with the objects of your perception? Disappearing takes practice. One method is to use your own breath. It is readily available and tax free. Breath can be a medium for prana (energy) and consciousness to fill you.

With the deepest relaxation your whole body opens itself to receive prana. When your breath combines with consciousness it becomes pure prana. Prana is the consciousness; and the breath is the manifestation. When you combine breath with consciousness it creates union. Energy and consciousness.

When you have nothing left to do or accomplish what is begins to emerge. The intersection of cosmic consciousness and your consciousness occurs when you give yourself permission to simply be present. Even for a moment it brings you to a space of unity.

The science of breath work is known as pranayam. This is two words. Prana, we know is energy. Ayam means regulate, or suppress. With breath work you regulate the vital energy of the body. Pranayama destroys that which covers (our emotions, thoughts and ego) the light. The promise of pranayama is to clarify the mind and balance the emotions. To still the fluctuations of the mind.

EXERCISE

Connect with the Energy of Sound

I sometimes hear yoga students (and teachers) chanting OM incorrectly. Like OHmmmm. Sort of like "home" with a big O in front. The sound is really closer to "aum". If you say it out loud, slowly, you may notice that the energy of this sound actually moves through your body from the base of your spine up through your chest and towards the top of your skull. That's what OM is supposed to do. Move energy up through your central nervous system in a combination of cleansing and receptivity.

Chant OM for two minutes. Be quiet and still. Experience the vibrations of the sound you have made. Experience the impact of the energy. Watch your breath. Don't control it. Observe. As the breath moves into your body simply acknowledge that consciousness is riding on top of the breath. Like a surfer on a wave. Don't worry about what the consciousness is supposed to mean. Don't give it definition. It comes in with the breath. Imagine that the breath is not only moving in and out of your lungs. It is moving, as it does, into all parts of your body. Your body is filling with this consciousness and the energy that it rides on. Shiva and shakti moving into you.

Your breath is helping you relax. This is a space where you disappear. You are in unity with what is. In this experience you disappear to feel and experience the combined energy and consciousness of mantra. Mantras do have specific energetic purposes so you should *feel* what that is.

Separation Does Not Exist

B.K.S. Iyengar provides insight on the subtle nature of energy and the reason we separate ourselves. He stands on a stage in an auditorium at a Yoga Journal conference with one of his disciples. The young man is in yoga head stand position, sirsasana. I watch intently a few rows away. Iyenger moves one of the young mans legs. Upside down the foot is about at the level of Mr. Iyengar's head. B.K.S. adjusts the foot imperceptibly. Maybe half of one inch. He asks the young man if he notices a difference in the energy in his body. "Yes," is the reply. Through practice we become increasingly sensitive to the energy in our body and the energy around us. Iyengar comments on one essential aspect of separation. He notes, "When we go to sleep we are all the same. Then, when we wake, we separate ourselves."

This is significant. Duality has to have time to exist. When you are "*in the zone*", connected to source, you lose sense of time. You lose duality and achieve polarity. This also happens in the deepest levels of sleep. You disappear. Dreams are, for most people, an unconscious energy process. Prana kriya. The great yoga masters discovered four primary states of consciousness. They are:

Turiya – The fourth state, absolute consciousness
Prajna – Dreamless, deep sleep
Taijasa – Dreaming
Vaisvanara – Waking state, material world

We know the waking state because that is what we're in most of the time. The dreaming state of consciousness brings us to a state where our subconscious mind is allowed to operate. This is not always comfortable or even restful. Have you ever had a dream where someone is chasing you, or something bad is happening? You wake up more tired than when you went to bed. The dreamless state brings us closer to source. We disappear. That is where most people stop. Turiya, the fourth state of consciousness, is when your mind is deeply resting with theta brain waves. Yet you remain conscious.

This is the state of consciousness you move into with Yoga Nidra. You realign with that part of your being that is beyond your intellect. When you try to use your mind to create change that has not been accepted at the deepest level of your being you either fail or see limited success. You unconsciously fight yourself.

During Turiya you move through the subconscious mind. The shift in perspective empowers you to resolve perceived problems and habitual patterns at their root. You access the infinite field of cosmic consciousness where collective knowledge, creative solutions and skillful action arise. All of your chakras open up and your energy moves freely. Your consciousness can now work in harmony with your energy to realign to true source. Great masters enter this state at will. Yoga Nidra provides training wheels for the rest of us.

Love, Consciousness and Connection to Source

Unconditional love also provides an immediate connection to source. Through love everything is possible that is not possible through the medium of the mind. Love is, of course, a manifestation of energy and consciousness. When you channel love you directly transmit all of the properties that come with love to any of the four worlds – including yourself. The heart center is the center to access, receive and transmit personal love. The crown center is the center to access, receive and transmit universal love.

You can give and receive love. But you can not hold love. It is fluid, like water and energy. The force of love moves through you and you can direct it. But remember we do not own love. The moment love and ego connect it is no longer love. Ego, the mind, can easily put an artificial, self indulgent wrapper around love. "I will give you love as long as _____." Fill in the blank. That is not unconditional. Worse, you are transforming your relationship into an object for the mind. When a human turns a relationship into an object it is really a crime. You must see others as part of yourself if you desire love and healing. In love, accept everyone as they are. The same applies to yourself. When you fully accept yourself and take "I AM LOVED" into your body, your energy is restored.

If there is one aspect of the guru and disciple relationship that is extremely potent it is that of learning and experiencing unconditional love. Many Westerners have a difficult time understanding what benefit can come from bowing down at the feet of a guru and offering unconditional love. It creates a reaction that is something like, "Why should I do that?" That is exactly why you should.

The act of selfless devotion to god through reverence to a great teacher provides an opening to completely release your ego. You open your heart to a divine being whose only purpose is to help you access your own soul. What a gift you receive. This is not a challenge, it is an honor. That does not come close to describing the experiential aspect of love that occurs. The guru opens himself or herself up to energetically channel love directly back to you. The more love you give, the more you receive.

Love is a state of consciousness. Watch a child play in a state of unconditional love. They easily, ecstatically enter a state of unity with the objects of their perception. They become the butterfly, flower, falling leaves and snowflakes. They accept and emulate the energy of the objects of their awareness. Like a tuning fork, they reverberate with the frequencies they receive. Their bodies move fluidly in tune with this energy. They dance, laugh and shout. They are not aware of their state of consciousness because it encapsulates them. As a state of consciousness, love provides the space where you can awaken to your true purpose in life. You are both in service to and in synchronization with your heart. You don't have to think. You know.

You were a child. You know this space even if you don't play there regularly. Move from your thinking center to your feeling center. Feel the energy in your body. Feel your body as light. The goal of the soul in this life is to return to source. Be still and aware. Watch for the internal stillness. Love and joy follow.

Connect the Collective to the Cosmic

June 5th, 1989 an unnamed man stands in front of a column of tanks in Beijing. It is one day after the Chinese government's violent crackdown in Tiananmen Square. The man stands alone in the middle of the road as tanks approach. He holds two bags, one in each hand. The tanks remain motionless in a standoff between one man who symbolizes the rights of individuals, and metal tanks that represent a regime that is not overly concerned about individual rights. Jeff Widener of the Associated Press takes a photo from the sixth floor of the Beijing Hotel, almost half a mile away. The image reaches international audiences overnight.

We live in the most amazing period in human history. In less than one hundred years modern communications has transformed our collective consciousness into a space where we rapidly acknowledge events and experiences that happen to the world. Time and space continue to collapse around us. Simultaneously, events around the globe are interconnected and interdependent. We experience *global* financial crises, *global* warming, *global* health epidemics.

Geographic and political borders are irrelevant. We are all one. Events that shape lives around the world are created by mankind and driven by the collective consciousness. Industrialized nations have greater and faster impact on global conditions. These same countries have given their soul to the world. China, Russia, Japan, India...even the United States. The wisdom of our ancestors and today's great masters continue to shape our lives. Globalization is not only created by large, multi-national companies that set up factories around the world. It is also created by great teachers who, like seeds, land and plant their ideas in countries around the world. If individuals like Mahatma Gandhi and Martin Luther King can change history, so too can any country.

Change requires that we not only modify the tune we play; but that we find an entirely new song to sing. The process by which this happens collectively, globally, is identical to how we effect change individually. First we have to recognize habitual patterns. Why does any nation, or the world, repeat events that create starvation, oppression, intolerance, fear or war? External circumstances are always a reflection of internal perceptions. Ironically, thousands of years of wars representing millions upon millions of ghastly deaths have neither slowed the accelerated growth of the human species, nor made a significant improvement in the lives of the majority of the people who remain alive. Clearly something is amiss. What are we doing with all of our prana?

We must consciously create new patterns for human interaction that follow the harmony of the universe. Since this is the nature of the universe it only requires that we look, listen and act more carefully. We need to take collective experience and place it individually into the realm of the cosmic, intuitive consciousness. As we individually tune into the concord of the universe we will co-create harmonious solutions for the entire planet.

EXERCISE

Experience Your Dreamer

If you lived your entire life in a desert climate you might only know snow from a photograph. That is not an experience of snow. It doesn't tell you how it feels. What it's like to fall in the snow; create a snowman; shovel a driveway or fly down a mountain on a snowboard. You have to experience time and space in new ways to know how you can use these invisible mediums. Here is an exercise that can help you navigate time and space in a new way using your aura.

Sit about three feet from another person. Three feet prevents sexual energy from being involved in the exercise. You are The Dreamer. You are going to expand your own aura to hold space and time around the other person. This expansion beyond the person sitting in front of you opens a door to the next reality. Your friend is The Subject. They are going to look anywhere they want. They can look above you. Usually eye-to-eye is not recommended because that makes a connection, which is not what this exercise is about.

1. The Dreamer looks about three inches above The Subject's head
2. The Dreamer expands their aura. You do this by breathing out. On your out breath feel your aura, your energy body, encompass The Subject. Keep your tongue on your palate to keep the energy connected and moving through your body. See if you can move your energy body around The Subject.

That may enough of an exercise to sense how you can energetically move through space and time in a new way. Try it with the four worlds. Your pets, plants, minerals. See what you can learn. Practice using your own spirit. Then you can move through time and space in new ways. It is one reason people meditate. During meditation you are not physically moving at all. You eliminate space. Your sense of time then is related to the meditation. When your mind leaves the stage you connect to spirit.

Know Time and Space

For me one of the great mysteries of human existence comes in the experience and perception of time and space. It is a dimension that is fluid and changing. Have you noticed that time not only does not stand still; but your perception of how fast it moves varies from moment to moment. One hour feels like an eternity. Another disappears like a heartbeat. And, during dreams, time is as elastic as the dreams themselves. The perception of the movement of time is directly related to the perception of the viewer.

The cheetah scorches across the open prairie with a top speed of seventy miles per hour and can go from rest to top speed in less than three seconds. A three-toed sloth, usually found hanging upside down in rainforests, creeps along at about seven feet per minute. By the time it has moved the length of an average sofa, the cheetha has zipped past a mile. Their experience of time and space is quite diverse.

We all live in the same space and time; but we experience it differently. Just as there is individual, collective and cosmic consciousness so too there is individual, collective and cosmic time and space. As the human race moves ever faster the collective perception of time and space continues to compress. A hundred years ago it was science fiction to consider a human walking on the moon. Today we see razor sharp images of Titan, the largest of Saturn's thirty three moons, on our computer screen.

Titan floats 744 million miles away from Earth. It took NASA's Cassini spacecraft four years to reach Saturn. Yet, traveling at the speed of light, images from the Huygens probe, which reached the surface of Titan after being launched from Cassini, give us crystal clear images of the moon. We can see drainage channels, a shoreline, flooded regions surrounded by elevated terrain and large ice boulders. How long? It takes an hour and twenty four minutes. Less time than is generally recommended to arrive at the airport before your plane leaves. Science changes our collective perception of space and time.

The human mind is a huge filter for the perception of space and time. It is another reason that being present in the moment is a critical aspect of awareness. When your mind is wandering along with thoughts of the past or projections of the future you are a time traveler. What else can you call it? If you're not totally here, right now, then where are you? Unfortunately your internal dialog presents only a vague, dreamlike catalog of what was or what might be.

Time and space are mediums for personal experience and growth. Like your soul, time and space are infinite. How can you use these fluid mediums to change your own reality and realize your intentions? One way is to eliminate them entirely from the equation.

It is why Shamans have learned to dream through time. Why yogis have learned that polarity arrives when time disappears. Consider this. If you had all the time in the world, endless like a vampire, would your view of your life and your activities change? If you find yourself saying, "I've always wanted to do such and such. If I had time I could do that."

You do have time. Time does not create a bucket list where you have to get a to-do list crossed off before you die. Realize your dream at this very moment. Walk in the space that you are holding in your intentions. Time is not an enemy that works against you. This is a misperception. Time is your friend. It is here, and it is endless.

In the realm of spirituality time has little meaning. How long does it take to know yourself? It is as ridiculous to imagine that you need twenty more lifetimes as it is to think transformation is not happening now. Take time off the table, out of the equation; and see how your life evolves. It is not a race. Take your time.

Notes and Experiences